EGYPTIAN TREASURES

Photographs by Seth Joel

Introduction by Michael Botwinick, Director, The Brooklyn Museum

Commentaries by Robert S. Bianchi, Associate Curator, Department of
Egyptian and Classical Art, The Brooklyn Museum

EGYPTIAN TREASURES

From the Collections of The Brooklyn Museum

Harry N. Abrams, Inc., Publishers, New York

Project Editor: Robert Morton
Editor: Margaret Donovan
Designers: Nai Chang and Gilda Kuhlman

Library of Congress Catalogue Card Number: 78-73468
International Standard Book Number: 0-8109-2170-7

Published in 1978 by Harry N. Abrams, Incorporated, New York

Printed and bound in Japan

On the Cover:

Profile Face Used as an Inlay

From the trench in the Great Temple at Tell el Amarna
Dynasty XVIII, time of Queen Nefertiti, 1357–1353 B.C.
Red quartzite
Gift of the Egypt Exploration Society, 33.685
The Brooklyn Museum
11.8 cm. (4⅝") in height

This elegant stone relief sculpture probably depicts Akhenaten's wife, the great Queen Nefertiti. The thrust of the chin, the full, pursed lips, the distinctive buccal muscle along the cheek—all suggest that beautiful and powerful woman.

The inlay, once probably set into a wall in a composition like a jigsaw puzzle, was discovered at Tell el Amarna, the capital of Egypt founded by Akhenaten. Several of the buildings at that site were decorated with inlays of various colored stone, glass, and faience. This fragment, modeled in low relief, also shows traces of red paint on the lips; the crown and neck, now missing, were probably made of different colored materials. So elaborate was the technique of Amarna artisans that even this inlay was probably further inlaid for decorative and realistic effect: here, the eye and brow were filled with contrasting substances. This sophistication indicates the high level of artistic attainment reached during the Amarna Period.

On Egyptian Art

There is a saying in Egypt, "Men fear time, but time fears the pyramids." This rather melodramatic sentiment carries within it one of the operative elements of the greatness of Egyptian civilization. It is not simply that the monuments of Ancient Egypt survive—they were built to survive—but that the civilization, as an active, living reality, endured for so long. A span of five thousand years is nearly beyond our comprehension. Yet, that, more or less, is the incredible life-span of Ancient Egypt.

We must approach a civilization this durable with admiration. Even as it had its ups and downs, it had an amazing power to survive. And while its forms were not immutable, its longevity suggests that basic to this civilization were certain elements that held it together for millennia. Its institutions clearly had the flexibility to modify and adapt themselves with changing times, and yet deep enough roots to retain their essential character over thousands of years. After all, some twenty dynasties and more than 1,500 years of pharaohs only bring us to the Biblical time of Moses and the Exodus of the Jews. And there was still a long way to go.

This vast span of time allowed for the growth of a complex social system. Here was a sophisticated civilization, not a simple undifferentiated society. Its cornerstones were the king, the priests, the nobility, and the farmers. Over the generations, complicated formulas evolved to regulate the relationships of the classes. Notice that the fourth component was farmers—not slaves. True, to work the land in Ancient Egypt was arduous and cruel. But the great labor force of Egypt was the farmer or peasant of the land. Theirs were the hands that built the pyramids. In the times of year when the level of the Nile made agriculture impossible, the people of the land comprised a vast public work force.

We are fortunate to have so much evidence of Ancient Egypt. Though it was a civilization of few known cities, it produced much art and much writing. Its commitment to permanence involved the construction of elaborate tombs and temples. In spite of thousands of years of depredations these tombs continue to be the source of much of our knowledge of Ancient Egypt. The temples survive as they were meant to survive. Built of the most durable materials, they were not intended as places of worship for the generation that erected them, but rather as the homes of gods and as the seats of creation.

Egypt's arid climate has helped to preserve much. The ever-productive soil seems to yield an infinite crop of antiquities sown industriously over the 5,000-year history of this culture. It is ironic that this constant crop is, at times, too rich for us to absorb and care for adequately and too often comes to us removed from its context, leaving us guessing about its meaning and use.

The geography of Egypt was as much a building block of its ancient civilization as its social system. Situated at the northeast corner of Africa, a bridge to the Levant and the Near East, it was inevitably a crossroads, an interconnector between Mesopotamia, Palestine, Syria, Crete, and Greece. The Nile forms the spine of the country, and the cycle of its annual flooding, which carried rich silt into the fields along its banks, literally gave life to the civilization. The Roman historian Herodotus could not have been more accurate when he said, "Egypt is the gift of the Nile." This mighty river gave the people of Egypt their sense of fatalism in the face of the greatness of natural forces. (It is a quality that runs deep in the national character even today. The present people of Egypt must in many ways reflect the ancient Egyptians not only in their fatalism, but in their humor, kindness, and patriotism.)

The reality of the Nile also contributed much to the philosophy and religion of Ancient Egypt. The river's constant cycle of renewal governed Egypt both physically and spiritually and engendered a philosophy of rebirth. We can see this in the Osiris myth. Osiris, whose story may be related to the legendary history of a real king, was slain by his jealous brother and the parts of his dismembered body were scattered over the earth. But Osiris's devoted wife, Isis, collected all of the parts and achieved his resurrection. Meanwhile, Horus, the son of Osiris and Isis, defeated his evil uncle and ruled Earth in his father's place; the restored Osiris became king of the Netherworld. By extension from the myth, every successive living king of Egypt ruled as Horus, and when he died, became Osiris as his own son replaced him on the throne as Horus. And the cycle is renewed, again and again. In the repetition of the cycle there is permanence, and in permanence, there is preservation.

We are once again led back to the internal Egyptian awareness of the longevity of their own civilization. The ongoing cycle, always repeating itself, carries the culture forward into time. Its monuments and its institutions, whether they be principles of kingship or rites of mummification, are all designed with the notions of permanence and preservation in mind. The impetus to preserve the body is the same one that fills tombs with meticulously carved sculptures and painted scenes of daily life to provide eternal diversion for the being in the Netherworld.

It is important to remember that art was not simply art for the ancient Egyptians. The objects we appreciate and classify as high art were in fact an integral part of existence in the ancient world. These objects were extensions of the culture, and the artist was but one of the artisans within the system. In a society in which there was no real separation between the religious and the secular, no differentiation between the reality of life here and now and life in the hereafter, the artifacts we label as art were utilitarian objects of a unified cosmography.

Art in Ancient Egypt must also be seen as an extension of writing. In a culture whose essential writing is pictographic, it is hard to determine where writing leaves off and art begins. But it is not critical to find the exact borderline. If our modern eyes are more comfortable classifying the vast majority of Egyptian pictorial representation as "Art," there is little we can do to escape the imprint of our own time. In the end, however, the eloquence of Egyptian relief—whether it is hieroglyphs pressed into a clay tablet, graven on tomb walls or temple pillars, inked on papyrus, cast on gold, or carved in stone sculptures—speaks to us no matter how we classify it.

It should come as no surprise that the forms, content, and uses of Egyptian art were as complex as the structure of Egyptian society. While, on the one hand, we can see hieroglyphs evolve into art, we can also see many examples of art as a simple reproduction of nature. This naturalism flourished at several times in the history of Egypt, peaking perhaps most vividly in the Amarna Period under Akhenaten, the pharaoh who briefly turned Egypt toward a kind of monotheism. But there was always an interest in beauty, though the ideal might vary. And, equally, the Egyptian artist was ever curious about details—the cut of a man's clothing, the design of a bit of jewelry, precisely how an animal

moves. We are too often exposed to certain hieratic images from Egyptian art. It has left us with a notion of sameness, a notion that is enhanced by the persistence in Egypt of certain basic institutions and motifs. But this persistence is not repetition; it is recurrence. There is a great variety in detail and style between kingdoms and even between individual rulers—as many of the objects in this book will show. These variations are of great help to art historians, who are often able to differentiate between objects and to date them solely on the basis of these stylistic differences.

If there is a quality that most Egyptian art shares, it is the way in which the artist conceives the reality of the subject he portrays in the object he produces. The Egyptian artist seeks a representation of what is seen in essence, not in a transitory or emotional moment. As such, Egyptian art is neither impressionistic nor expressionistic. It captures a higher level of reality of the subject. Whether in a painting of a noblewoman, a statue of a pharaoh, or a faience figure of a baboon, the artist provides all the details and elements that are essential to see the totality of the subject.

We should avoid thinking of Egyptian art as the product of a distant, long-dead civilization. Much time, it is true, has passed since its creation. But the record left behind is vivid; it speaks of beauty, triumph, pride, celebration, struggle, loss, sorrow, strength, death, and—above all—of life.

Since the first recorded acquisition in 1902 of objects from Ancient Egypt, the collection of Egyptian art at The Brooklyn Museum has grown to be, not among the largest, but certainly among the finest, in the world.

Parallel with the growth of the Museum, interest in the art and archaeology of Ancient Egypt grew rapidly in Brooklyn. As early as 1906, the Museum conducted a successful survey of Predynastic sites in Upper Egypt that resulted in the acquisition of several unique examples that go back to the end of the fifth or the beginning of the fourth millennium B.C., centuries before the "dawn of history." It received its first mummy and first coffin in 1908 when the Egyptian collection of Armand De Potter was acquired. In 1915, many Coptic textiles were obtained from the excavations of the Egypt Exploration Fund at Antinoöpolis. This acquisition marked the beginning of what has grown to be probably the most extensive assemblage of Coptic art in this country. It was 1916, however, that was a real milestone in the history of the Museum, for it was then that the library and collection of Charles Edwin Wilbour were given to the Museum by his children.

Charles Edwin Wilbour was born in Little Compton, Rhode Island, in 1833. He attended Brown University, was admitted to the bar, became a court reporter in New York, and then publisher of *The (New York Daily) Transcript*—the only daily legal newspaper of his time. Following setbacks in his political career, Wilbour sailed for Europe, where he resumed his earlier studies in the humanities and began specializing in the new academic field of Egyptology. After attending courses in France and Germany—and avidly collecting books on Ancient Egypt—he went to Egypt, and from 1880 until his death in 1896, he spent every winter on the Nile, visiting the monuments, collecting artifacts, and studying inscriptions.

A man of wide learning, Wilbour was greatly respected by his colleagues in Europe and in Egypt, and his library must have been one of the finest private libraries of the time. When it came to Brooklyn, it contained nearly every nineteenth-century publication on Ancient Egypt. From twenty-five hundred volumes in 1916, it has grown tenfold and is now one of the best Egyptological libraries anywhere. Wilbour also assembled over two thousand antiquities, and part of this collection came to the Museum in 1916. However, it was 1947 before the Museum received the outstanding portion of his collection, which included Aramaic papyri of the fifth century B.C. that had been found at Elephantine, folded and sealed just as they had been filed away over two thousand years ago. It is the largest single collection of its kind in the Western World.

The bequest in 1931 of the residuary estate of Wilbour's only son, Victor, saw the establishment of the Charles Edwin Wilbour Fund, the income from which was to be used for "the purpose of maintaining and adding to and developing the Egyptological Collection and library." This important endowment enabled the Museum to install the Wilbour Collection, together with Egyptian objects from other sources, and, most important of all, permitted the Museum to engage a staff able to fulfill the terms of Victor Wilbour's bequest—predecessors of the present highly qualified curatorial staff of the Department of Egyptian and Classical Art.

Another major development in the history of Egyptian art at The Brooklyn Museum began with the arrival, in 1937, of some two thousand antiquities on indefinite loan from the New-York Historical Society. In 1948 this remarkable collection, reflecting almost every aspect of Egyptian art, was purchased for the Museum's permanent collection.

The reputation of The Brooklyn Museum as a major repository of fine works from Ancient Egypt is founded on a continuing history of important loans, gifts, bequests, and purchases, and is demonstrated by its active contribution to increasing awareness and knowledge of Egyptian art through its program of major international exhibitions.

Michael Botwinick
Director, The Brooklyn Museum

1. Statuette of a God

Provenance not known
Dynasty III, 2635–2570 B.C.
Gneiss
Charles Edwin Wilbour Fund, 58.192
The Brooklyn Museum
21.3 cm. (8³⁄₈″) in height

This figure is one of the earliest known stone sculptures of an Egyptian deity in human form. He wields a dagger in his right hand and clenches his left fist. Wearing a globular wig and an uncommonly long ceremonial beard, the deity is clad in a penis sheath, a garment thought to have been made of leather and apparently a traditional costume among male Libyans of the time. On the basis of his costume, scholars conjecture that this statuette represents the god Ha, who is called "The Master of Libya and the Lord of the West."

The dating of this representation of the god Ha is based on certain details of the costume, the material of the sculpture, and the curved top of the slab against which the figure stands. Careful attention to these features and comparisons among them and those of other works have enabled art historians to establish relative dates for many similar objects which may have been long removed from their archaeological contexts.

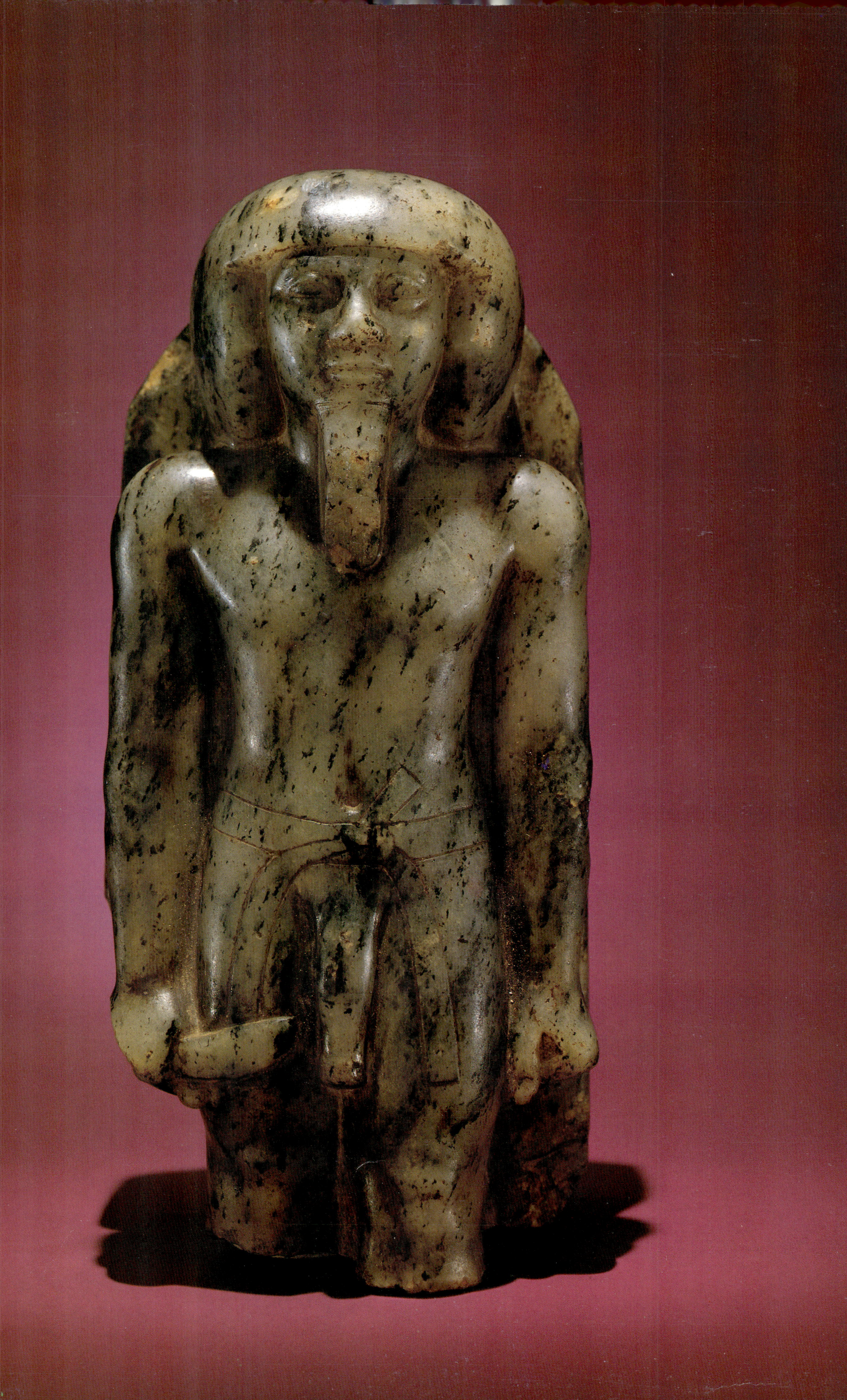

2. Seated Statue of Queen Ankhnes-mery-ra and Her Son Pepy II

Reportedly from Saqqara
Dynasty VI, 2251–2157 B.C.
Alabaster
Charles Edwin Wilbour Fund, 39.119
The Brooklyn Museum
39.2 cm. (15¹/₂″) in height

When the group of sculptures to which this object belonged first appeared on the art market, scholarly opinion of its proper period was sharply divided because of the prevailing notion that the Egyptian craftsmen of Dynasty VI never achieved such delicacy of composition, or created forms with the limbs cut free, or attained such luminosity with translucent alabaster. Today, the piece is ranked among the masterpieces from the late Old Kingdom.

The statue was commissioned to demonstrate the administrative ability of the child monarch Pepy II, whose early career prospered under the guidance of his mother, Ankhnes-mery-ra. Pepy II went on to have a reign of almost one hundred years, longer than that of any known monarch from Western Asia or the Classical lands. Here, the Queen holds her son on her lap in a pose that would later become the canonical motif for representations of the goddess Isis and her son Horus. This pose then passed into Christian iconography for representations of the Virgin Mary and Christ Child.

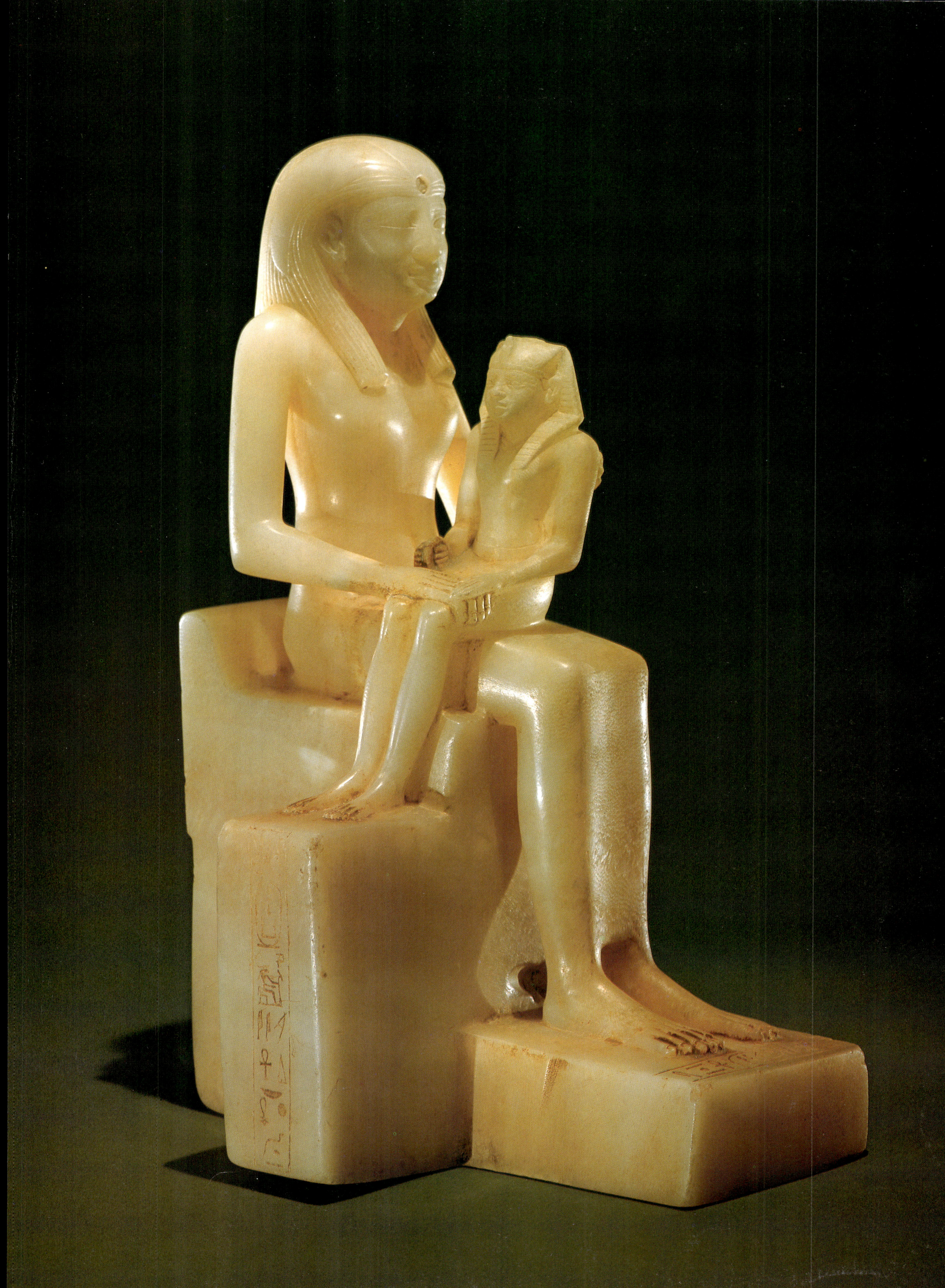

3. Seated Statue of King Sesostris III

Reportedly from Hieraconpolis
Dynasty XII, 1897–1878 B.C.
Black granite
Charles Edwin Wilbour Fund, 52.1
The Brooklyn Museum
54.5 cm. (21¹/₂″) in height

One of the cornerstones of the religion of the ancient Egyptians was their belief in the concept of *pars pro toto,* whereby a part of any given object could represent and act as if it were the entire object itself. In this powerful statue, King Sesostris III is represented wearing the tail of a bull attached to his belt. (It is visible between his legs.) By wearing the bull's tail, Sesostris becomes "The Strong Bull." A further symbol of his authority is that beneath the soles of his bare feet are representations of The Nine Bows, each representing one of the traditional foes of Egypt. Sesostris III thereby appears continually trampling the enemies of his country.

The pose of this sculpture depicts the king wearing a *nemes*-headcloth and striated kilt and holding an audience at court. Since these political sessions could become heated, he holds a bolt of cloth in his right hand with which to wipe his brow of sweat, a remarkably naturalistic and human touch. The unstable reign of Sesostris III and other kings of Dynasty XII, some of whom were assassinated, is underlined by the careworn expression of this monarch's face and by the protective amulet he wears suspended from his neck.

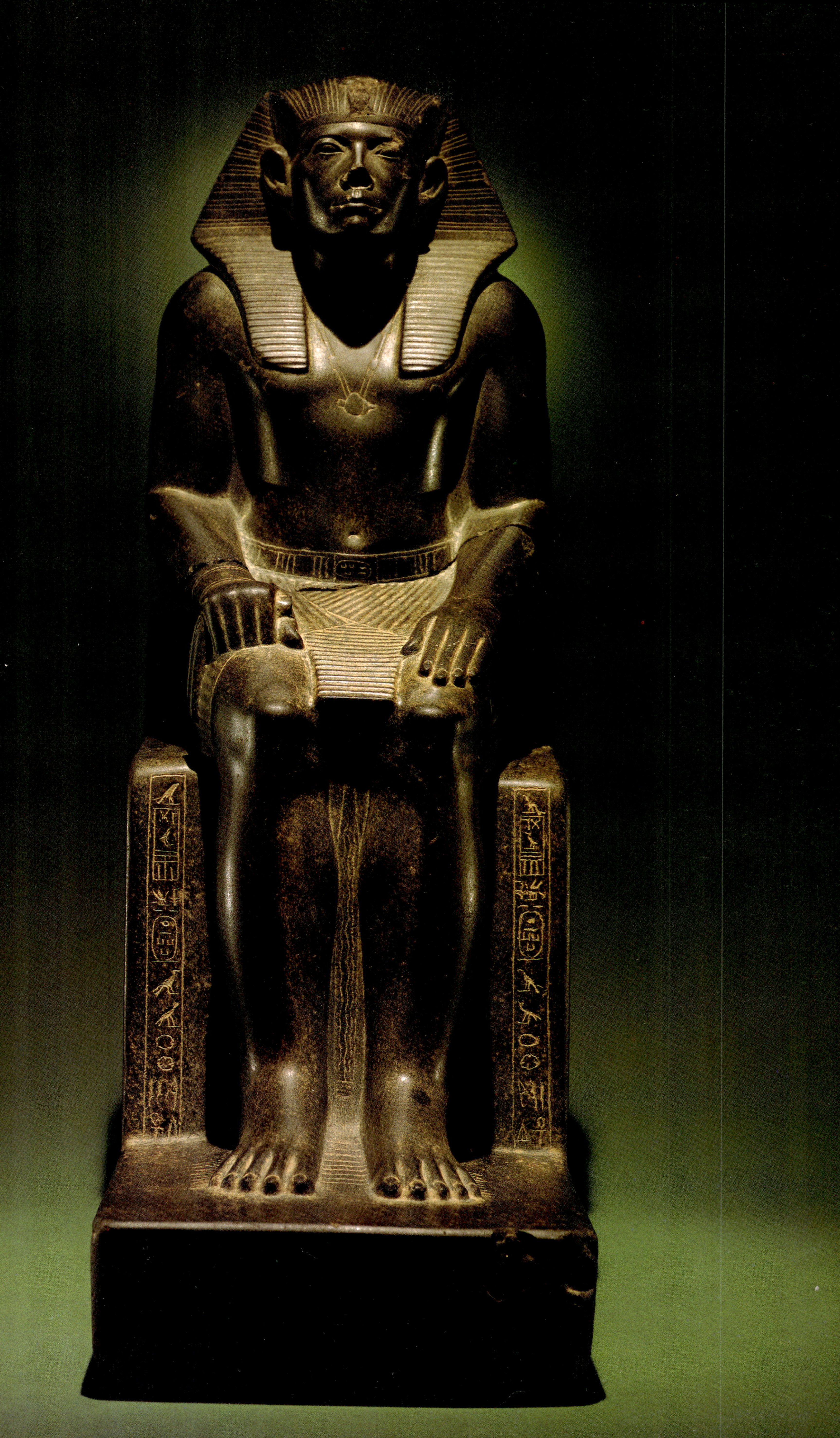

4. Gold Fly Necklace

Provenance not known
New Kingdom, Dynasty XVIII, 1554–1305 B.C.
Gold and lapis lazuli
Charles Edwin Wilbour Fund, 08.480.198
The Brooklyn Museum
21.7 cm. (8¹/₂") in length

Jewelry best exemplifies the inherent sense of design lavished by ancient Egyptian craftsmen on their work. In this example, a feeling of symmetry is achieved by the alternation of gold cylinder and ball beads with small but effective representations of the common housefly. The Egyptian love of strong color is achieved by combining the rich blue of lapis lazuli with reddish-yellow gold to achieve an uncommon brilliancy. The lapis lazuli probably came into Egypt as tribute from a Near Eastern dependency, which had obtained the stone from Afghanistan.

During Dynasty XVIII, the pharaohs of Egypt controlled huge areas of the Near East with their efficient armies. This necklace was probably worn by a valiant, high-ranking soldier: the housefly was a symbol of persistence, and an Egyptian soldier could be compared to a fly, which can harass its enemy with little risk of being either captured or killed.

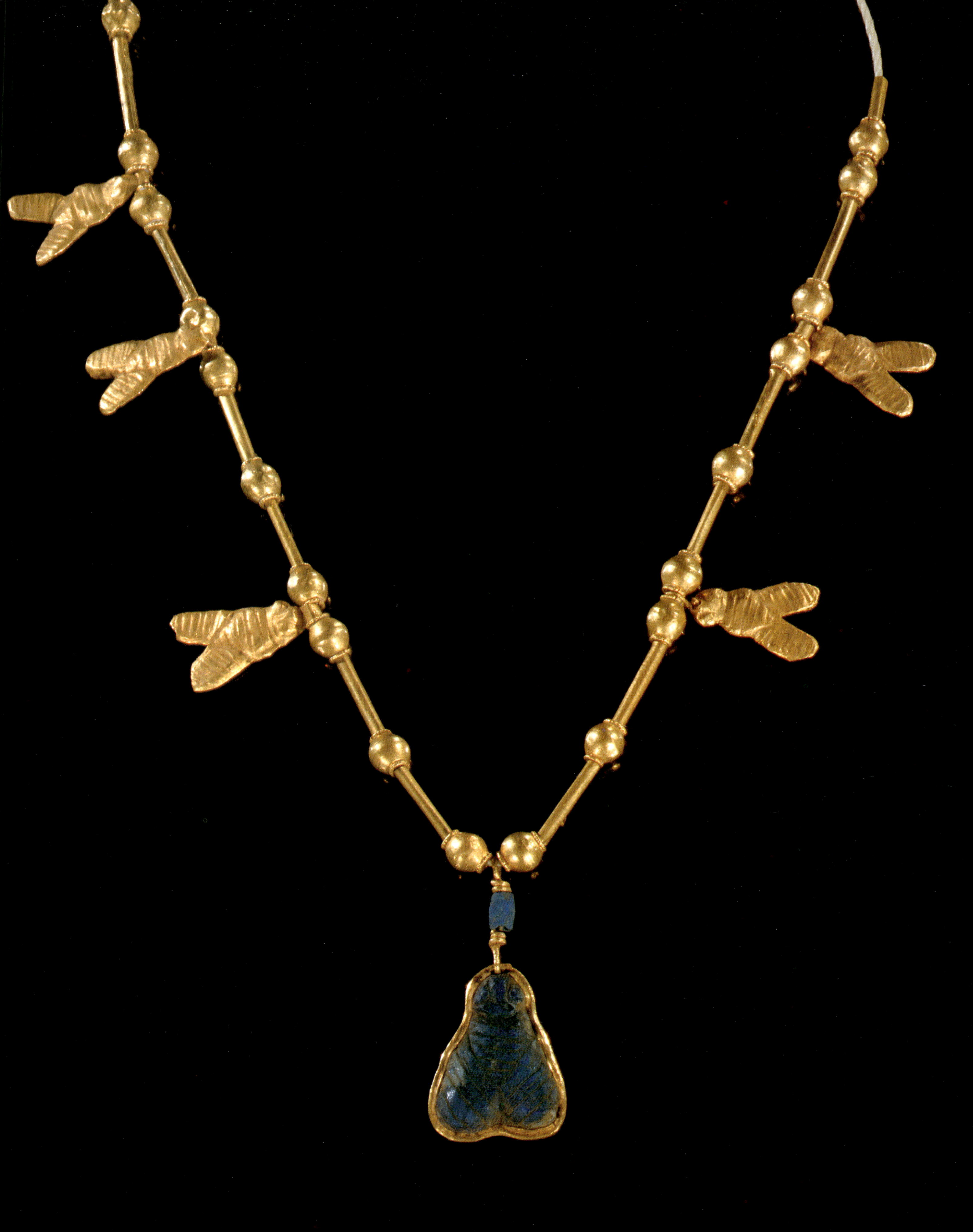

5. Shawabti of the Scribe Amenemhet

Thebes, Tomb no. 82
Dynasty XVIII, time of King Tuthmosis III, 1490–1436 B.C.
Painted limestone
Charles Edwin Wilbour Fund, 50.128
The Brooklyn Museum
24.5 cm. (9⅝") in height

The word "shawabti" is derived from the Egyptian hieroglyphs for "the one who answers." The function of these figures, which were buried in the tombs of important persons, was to answer the call to "move sands from the East to the West." This operation of the Afterlife, described in Chapter VI of *The Book of the Dead,* in which activities were very similar to those of the living world, required the conscription of the free population to toil on public works projects, particularly the maintenance of the irrigation canals so necessary for Egypt's agrarian economy. To facilitate this posthumous work, the shawabti carries hoes with which to work the earth and baskets with which to carry it away. So distasteful was even this imagined conscription, that before his death, the scribe Amenemhet ordered a set of shawabtis, one for each day of the year. To insure that each shawabti would work on his appointed day, Amenemhet commissioned an additional thirty-six figures of foremen to be included in the group! A contract written on papyrus has even survived outlining the terms by which the shawabtis and foremen would be manufactured.

This particular shawabti is remarkable for the excellent state of the paint's preservation. As a result, one can visualize what ancient Egyptian sculpture, almost all of which was painted, originally looked like. The hieroglyphs on the front contain the names and titles of Amenemhet as well as excerpts of Chapter VI of *The Book of the Dead.*

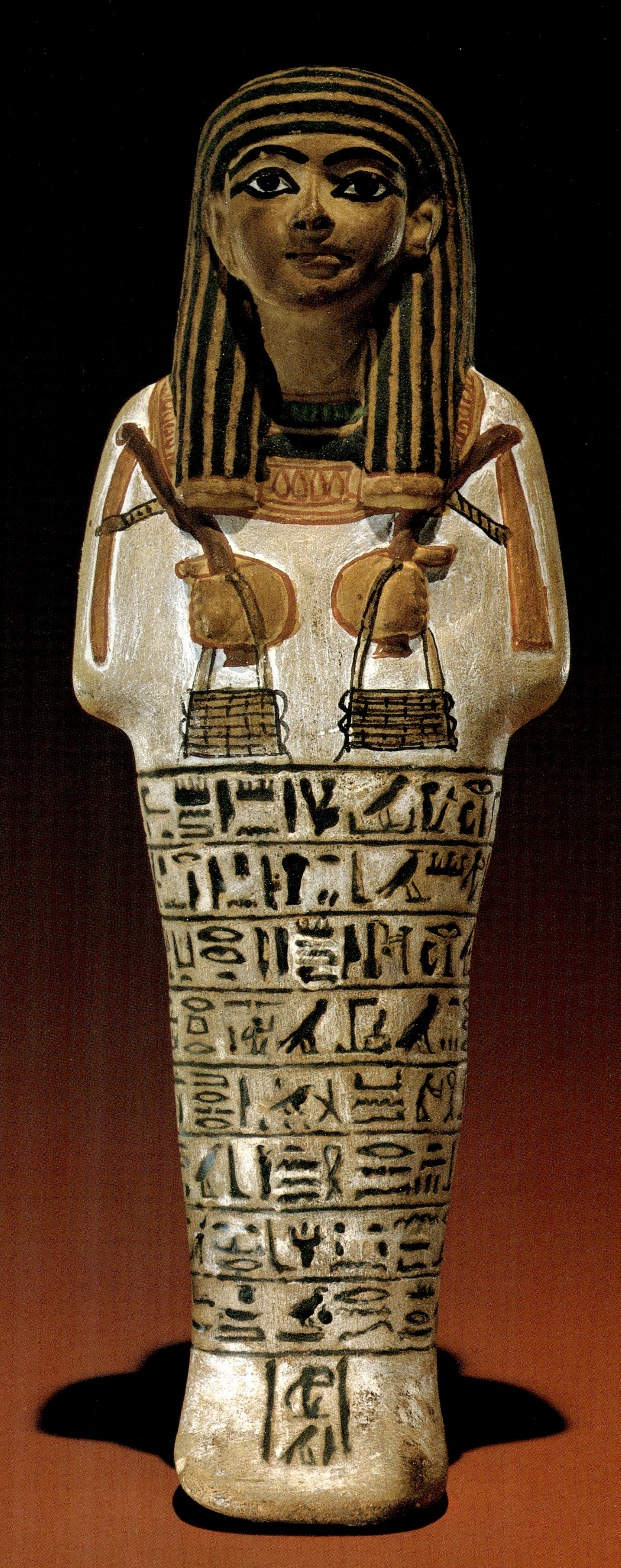

6. Pair Statue of Neb-sen and Nebet-ta

*Reportedly from Sumenu, near the modern village of Mahamid, eighteen
miles south of Luxor*
Dynasty XVIII, made in the time of King Amenhotep III, 1403–1365 B.C.
Painted limestone
Charles Edwin Wilbour Fund, 40.523
The Brooklyn Museum
40.4 cm. (15⁷/₈") in height

The strong family ties which the ancient Egyptians strove to maintain are
well illustrated in this sculpture. According to its inscriptions, it was
created in his parents' honor by a devoted son, Wesir-het, who apparently
had inherited his father's position as a scribe in the treasury of the king.
The father, Neb-sen, sits beside his wife, Nebet-ta, who was herself
distinguished as a chantress of the goddess Isis. Their mutual affection
is indicated by the symmetrical hugging of each other's shoulders.

Both husband and wife are shown wearing the very latest in Egyptian
fashion, which then tended to be unisex. Both wear elaborate wigs, broad
collars, and bracelets. Neb-sen also wears armlets and holds a bolt of
cloth. He is depicted with flaccid pectoral muscles and distinctive folds
of flesh on his chest and mid-section; these are artistic conventions to
indicate that he was not a manual worker but held an administrative
position. Inscriptions on the sculpture invoke various gods to grant
Wesir-het's parents a fine memorial and an everlasting supply of offerings.

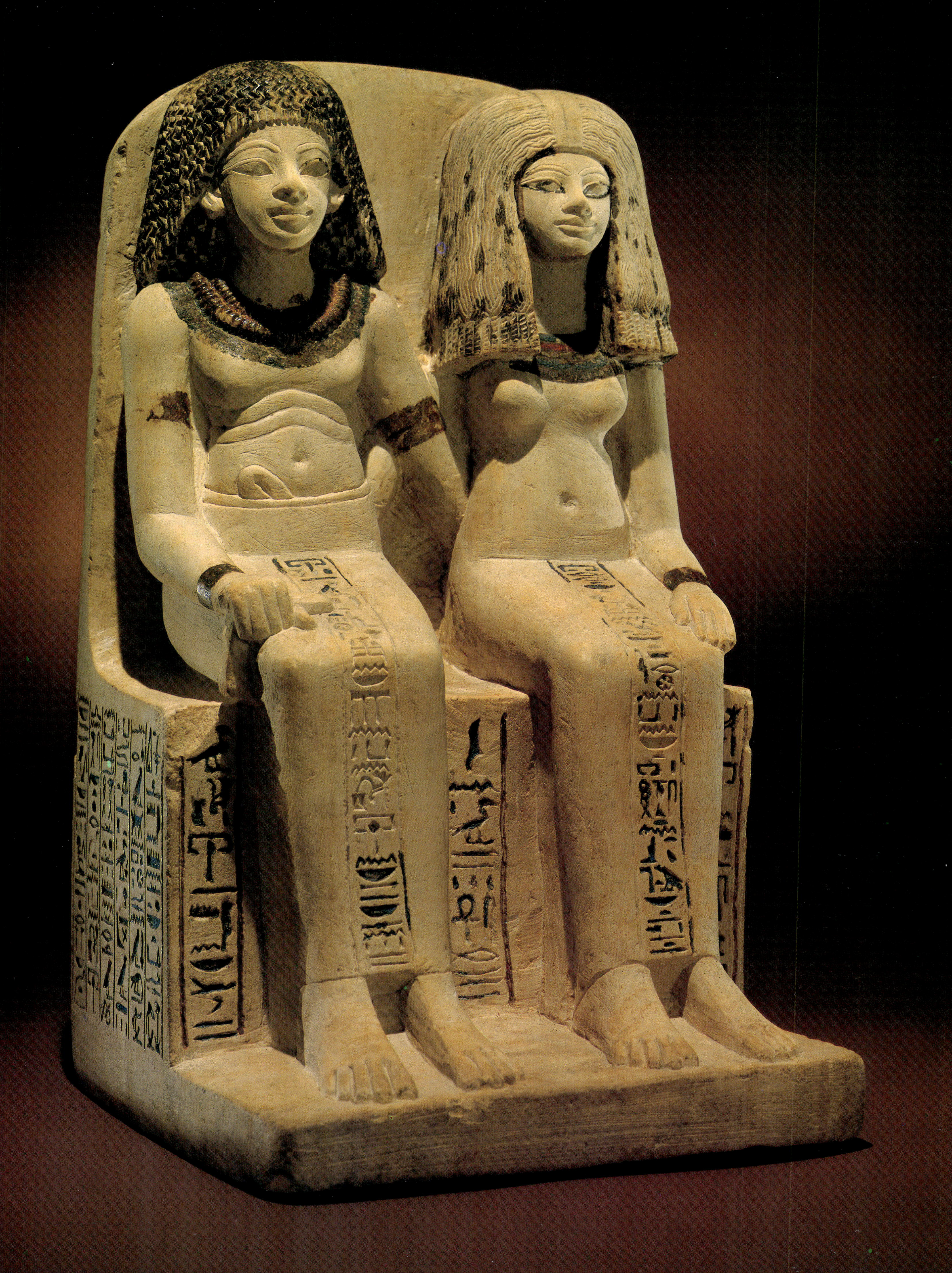

7. Figure of a Spoonbill

From the Palace of King Amenhotep III at Malkata, Thebes
Dynasty XVIII, 1403–1365 B.C.
Painted wood
The Tytus Collection, Gift of Mrs. Lawrence Coolidge and
Mrs. Robert Woods Bliss, 48.66.1
The Brooklyn Museum
9.7 cm. (3³/₄") in height

This charming bird, carved in wood and painted, has been identified as a
spoonbill, whose flocks were once plentiful throughout Egypt. The
spoonbill, whose pose here is very reminiscent of that of the American
flamingo, is, indeed, still found along the sandbanks of the Nile River and
in the great marshes of the Fayum and the Delta.

Representations of the spoonbill are rare; this example is one of only
two known to the author. Because of its rarity, the mythological associations
of the bird in Egyptian religion are not fully understood.

Here, however, the enchanting pose of the creature—verging on
caricature—is very appealing to modern sensibilities and could only have
been achieved during a period of Egyptian art that was dominated by a
strongly naturalistic movement. Although the exact purpose or function of
the figure remains unknown, there is some evidence to suggest that it
served as a child's toy.

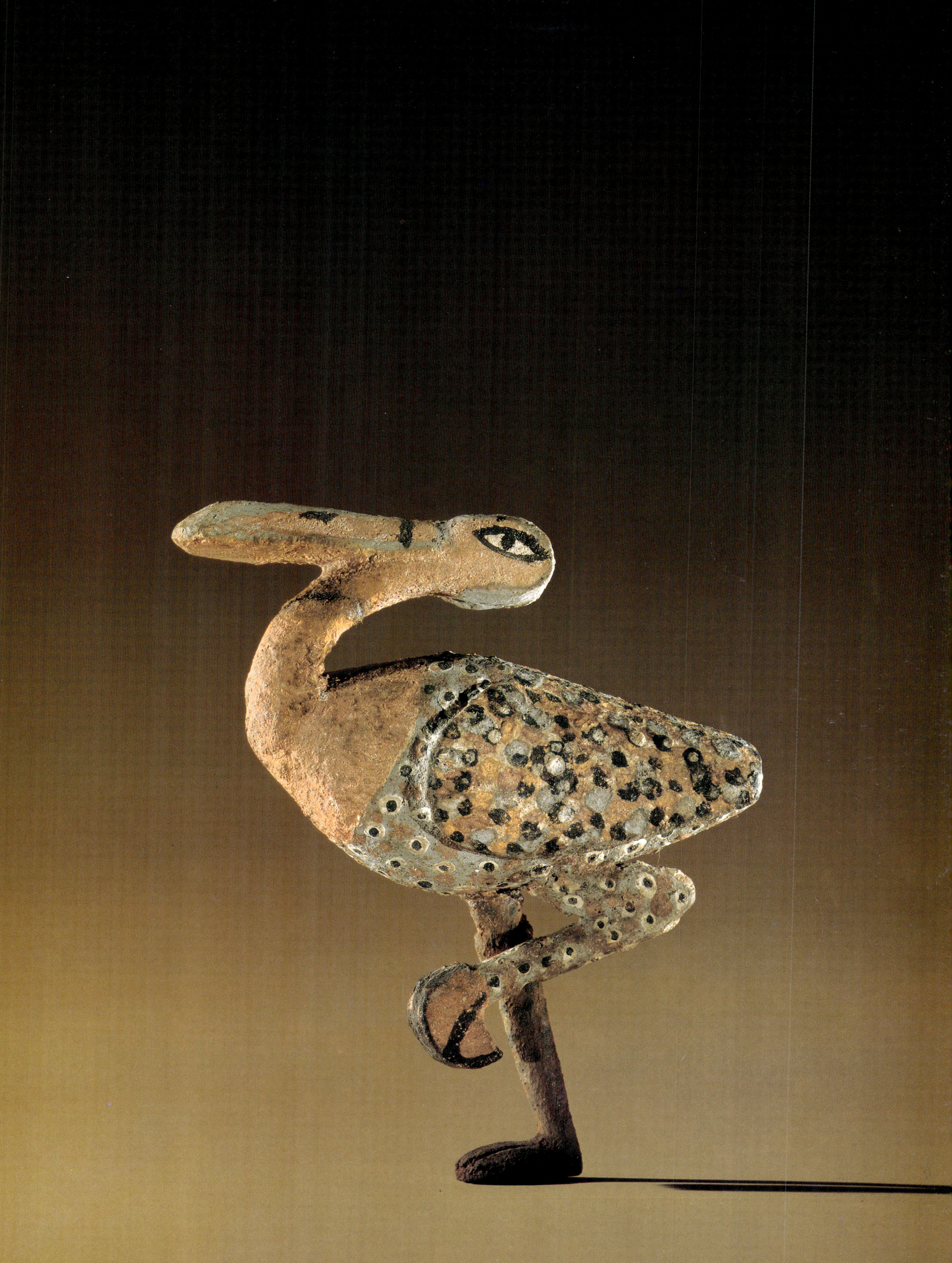

8. Representation of the Lady Thepu

From Thebes, Tomb no. 181
Dynasty XVIII, early in the time of King Amenhotep III, 1403 – 1365 B.C.
Paint on gesso over mudplaster
Charles Edwin Wilbour Fund, 65.197
The Brooklyn Museum
37.6 cm. (14³/₄") in height

This fragment of a wall painting comes from a tomb in the Theban
necropolis. The tomb is unusual since it was built not for an individual, but
for two men, the sculptors Nebamun and Ipuky. The lady pictured is Thepu,
Nebamun's spouse, although the word *hemit,* "wife," never appears in the
inscriptions on the walls of the tomb. Instead, Thepu is called *senet,* "[his]
sister," which was the fashionable word for "wife" during Dynasty XVIII.
Evidence that the identification is correct, however, includes traces of the
signs *p* and *u,* the last letters in Thepu's name, followed by the sign of a
seated woman in the upper right-hand corner.

Thepu is wearing a gala wig upon which is placed an ointment cone,
whose perfumed scent would fill the air around her. A broad collar, or
necklace, and a gossamer shawl seductively draped over her breast
contribute to the charming qualities of this portrait.

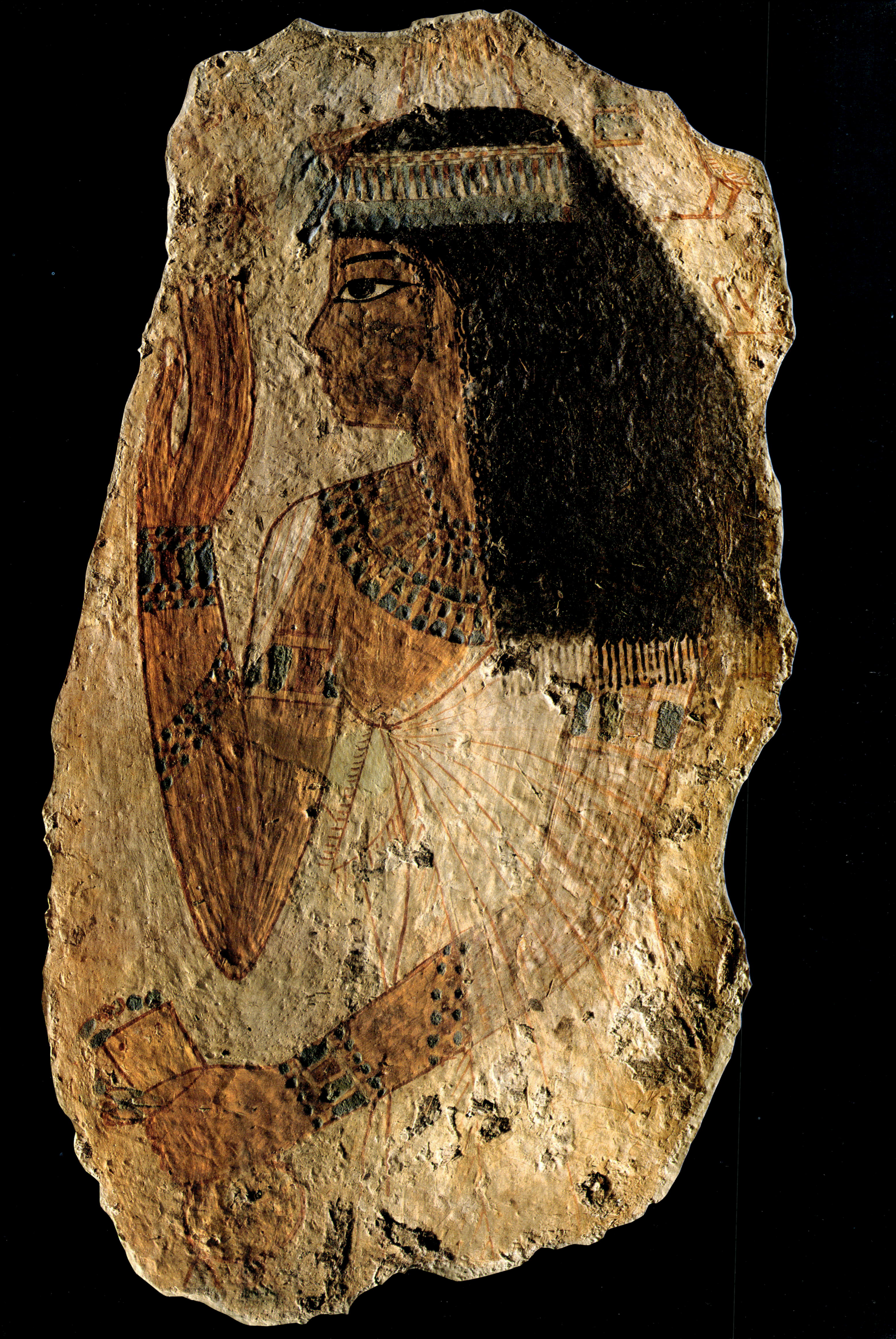

9. Statuette of a Nude Girl

Reportedly from the Tomb of Tutankhamen, 1347–1336 B.C.
Dynasty XVIII
Painted ivory
Charles Edwin Wilbour Fund, 40.126.2
The Brooklyn Museum
8.3 cm. (3¹/₄") in height

Some of the objects found in the sensational discovery of the tomb of Tutankhamen in 1922 were not made expressly for his burial but obviously had been handed down to him by his predecessors. This ivory figurine has a blue faience base on which is inscribed the name of King Amenhotep III (1403–1365 B.C.). Exceptional possessions such as this must surely have been handed from generation to generation as heirlooms. This practice would explain why this object, made perhaps twenty years before his birth, was finally associated with the funerary possessions of King Tutankhamen.

In any case, the figure most likely represents one of the numerous members of Amenhotep's harem. Her elaborate wig, thickly painted in black and topped by an ointment cone, her vivid red lips, and black pubic triangle, as well as the suggestive gesture of her left arm, evoke the erotic charms of the most attractive Egyptian courtesans. The effect of sensuality is heightened by the skill and care with which all the details of female anatomy are captured, even on this small scale; photographed in a mirror to show its three-dimensional qualities, the figure is less than three and a half inches tall.

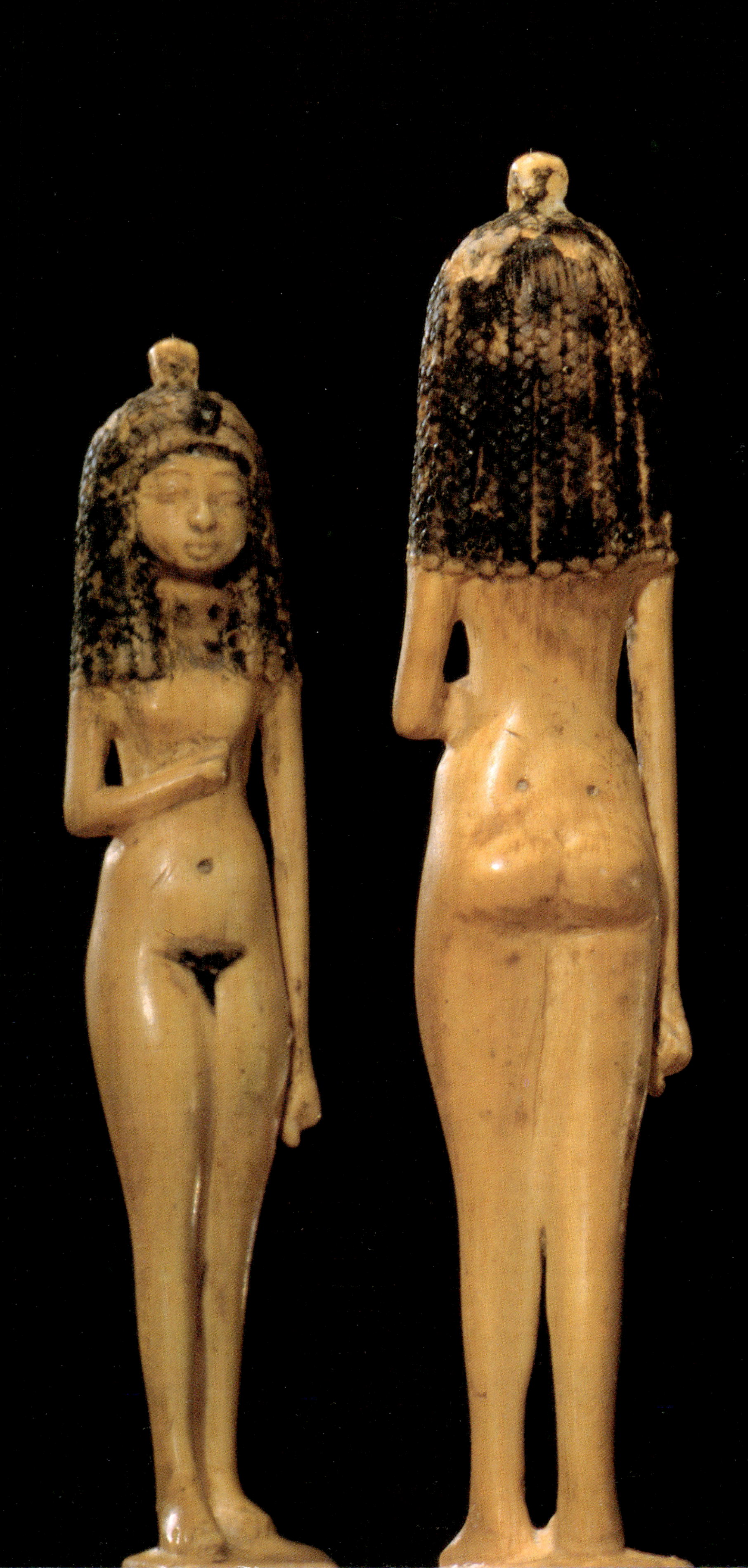

10. Inscribed Scarab

Provenance not known
Dynasty XVIII, time of King Horemhab, 1332–1305 B.C.
Gold
Charles Edwin Wilbour Fund, 37.715E
The Brooklyn Museum
1.8 cm. (⁵⁄₈″) in diameter

This finely crafted gold sculpture—less than three-quarters of an inch
long—is a detailed rendering of the dung beetle, whose Latin name,
Scarabaeus sacer, gave rise to the word "scarab," by which such
representations are universally called. The scarab itself is a hieroglyph,
pronounced *khepher,* which is used for the verb "to come into existence."
The ancient Egyptians had observed how the beetle would roll dung into a
ball, from which its larvae would hatch. They then equated the movement
of the sun across the sky with the action of the beetle's rolling. As a result,
the scarab became a symbol of rebirth.

Scarabs invariably have an oval-shaped, flat bottom used for
inscriptions, which suited them as amulets, seals, or commemorative
objects. This scarab is inscribed with the name of Mut-nedjem, the wife
of King Horemhab, the last ruler of Dynasty XVIII. It is one of just four
such gold scarabs known from that period. The hollow tube running the
length of the object under the beetle's legs presumably enabled it to be
mounted as a ring.

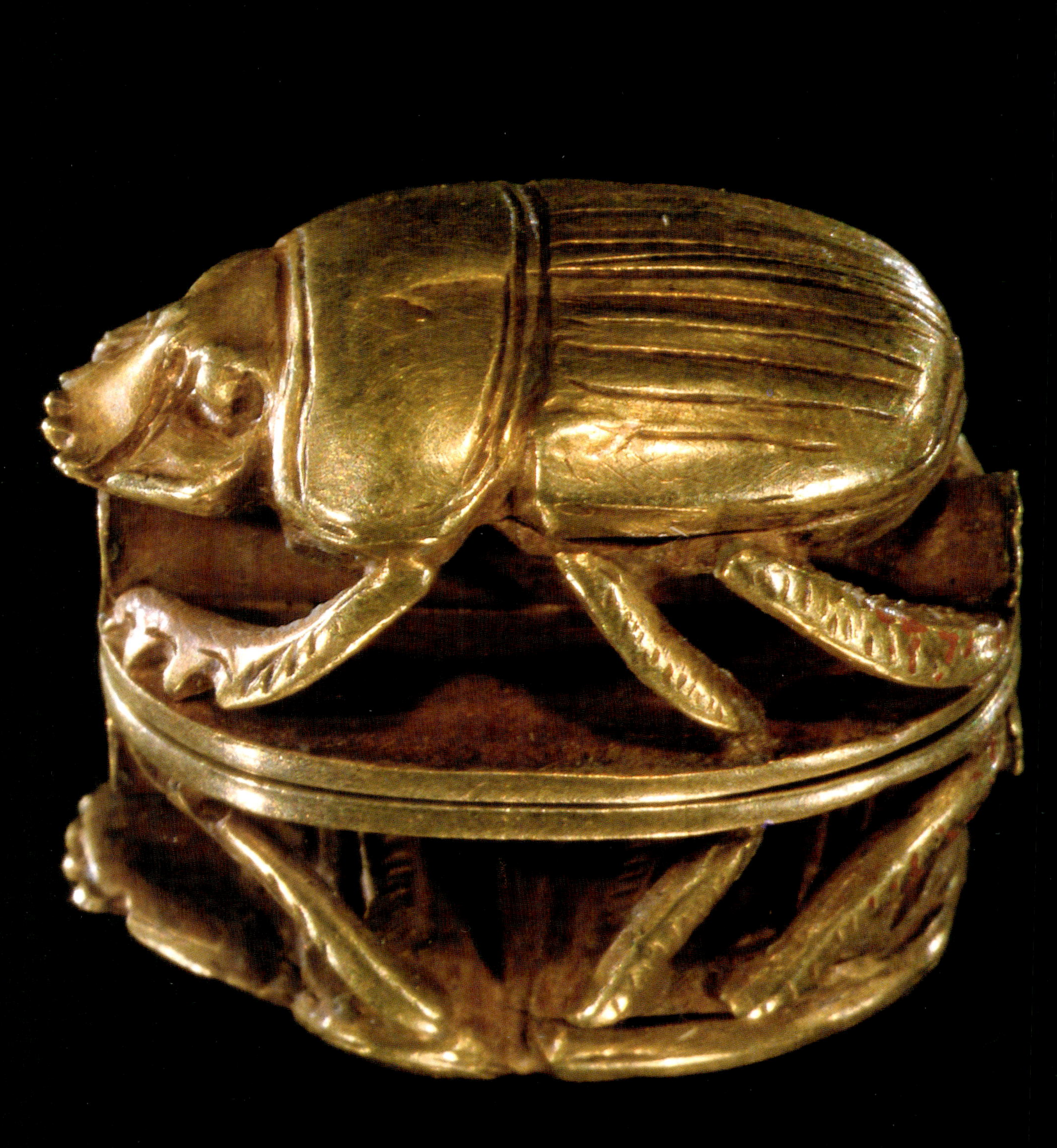

11. Block Statue of Yii

From Dahamsha, near Mahamid, north of Gebelein
Dynasty XVIII, time of King Ay, 1337–1332 B.C.
Indurate limestone
Charles Edwin Wilbour Fund, 66.174.1
The Brooklyn Museum
47.2 cm. (18⁵/₈″) in height

Block statues such as this—among the most frequently encountered types of Egyptian sculpture—are so named because their shapes and contours so clearly recall the blocks of stone from which they were worked. Some scholars maintain that this form was intentionally created as a visual expression for civilization's primeval mound rising from the abyss of chaos; others contend that the form was practical since statues of this type have a low center of gravity and were very stable when set up in tombs and temples.

Yii, the man depicted, served as second prophet of the god Amun, was first prophet of the goddess Mut, and also acted as a royal scribe. The inscriptions contain a prayer to the crocodile god Sobek-Ra and a greeting to Thoth, the god of writing. The cartouche, an oval representing a rope and enclosing the hieroglyphs for the name of King Ay on the upper surface of the right arm, provides the date for this statue.

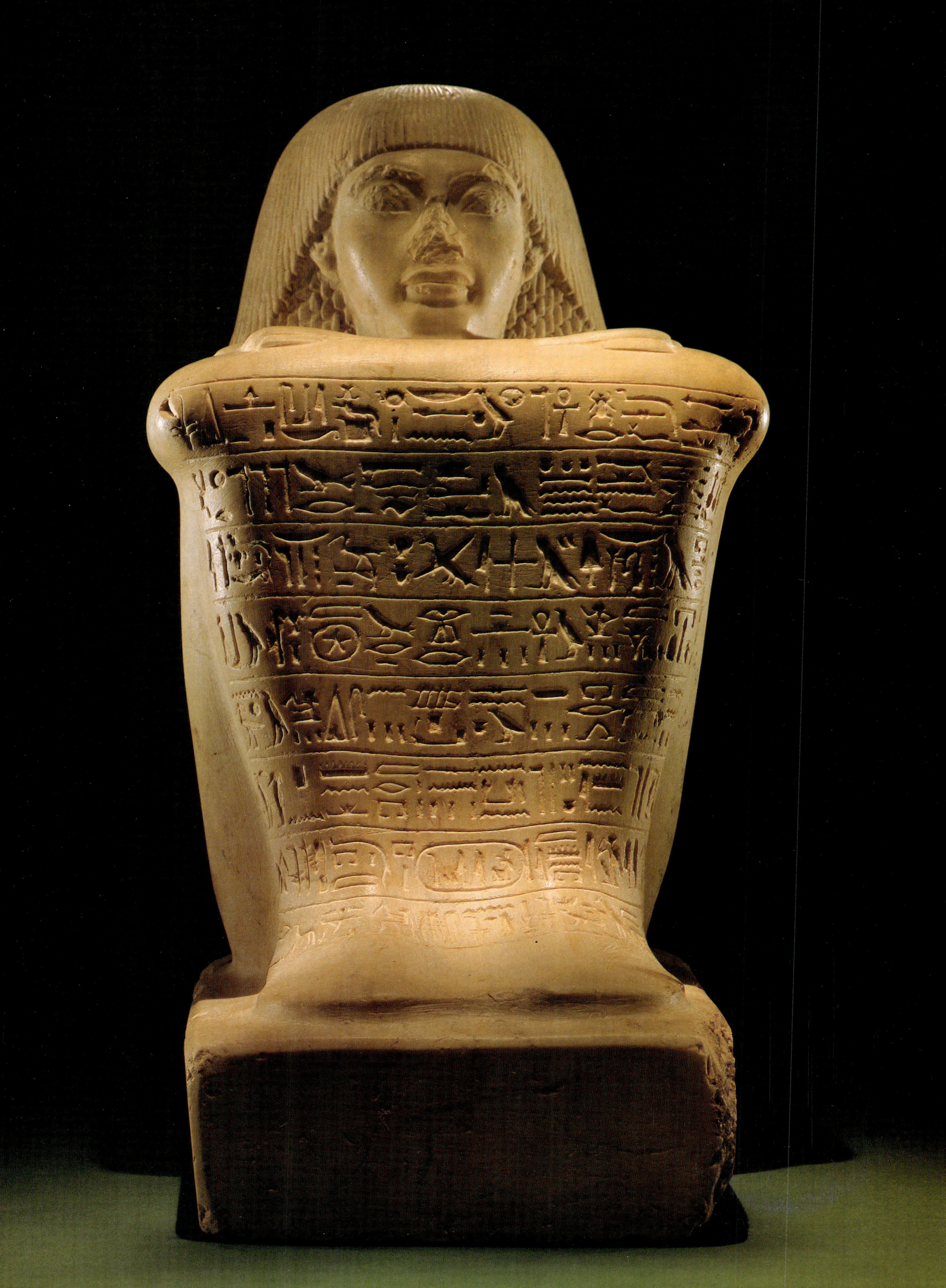

12. Figure of the God Tutu

Provenance not known
Dynasty XIX, 1305–1196 B.C.
Bronze
Charles Edwin Wilbour Fund, 61.20
The Brooklyn Museum
12.8 cm. (5") in height

In addition to the major deities of their pantheon, the ancient Egyptians
worshiped a great number of lesser beings who, nevertheless, exerted
considerable influence on their lives. One such being was Tutu, whose
name is still imperfectly understood. Tutu is represented as a composite
beast resembling a sphinx having a lion's body, a human head, a serpent as
a tail, and wings delicately etched into its back.

The ancient Egyptians considered Tutu to be the son of the goddess
Neith. When one invoked Neith in time of need, she would dispatch her son
Tutu to avert evil from the suppliant. Consequently, his standard description
is "The-one-who-keeps-foes-at-a-safe-distance."

This particular representation of Tutu is mounted on a base, suggesting
that it once was fastened to the top of a pole as a standard. Such standards
are often depicted in Egyptian wall paintings fixed to the prows of the
sacred boats of various deities. Tutu therefore served as the look-out for
the god and could command the serpents accompanying him to attack any
foe in his path.

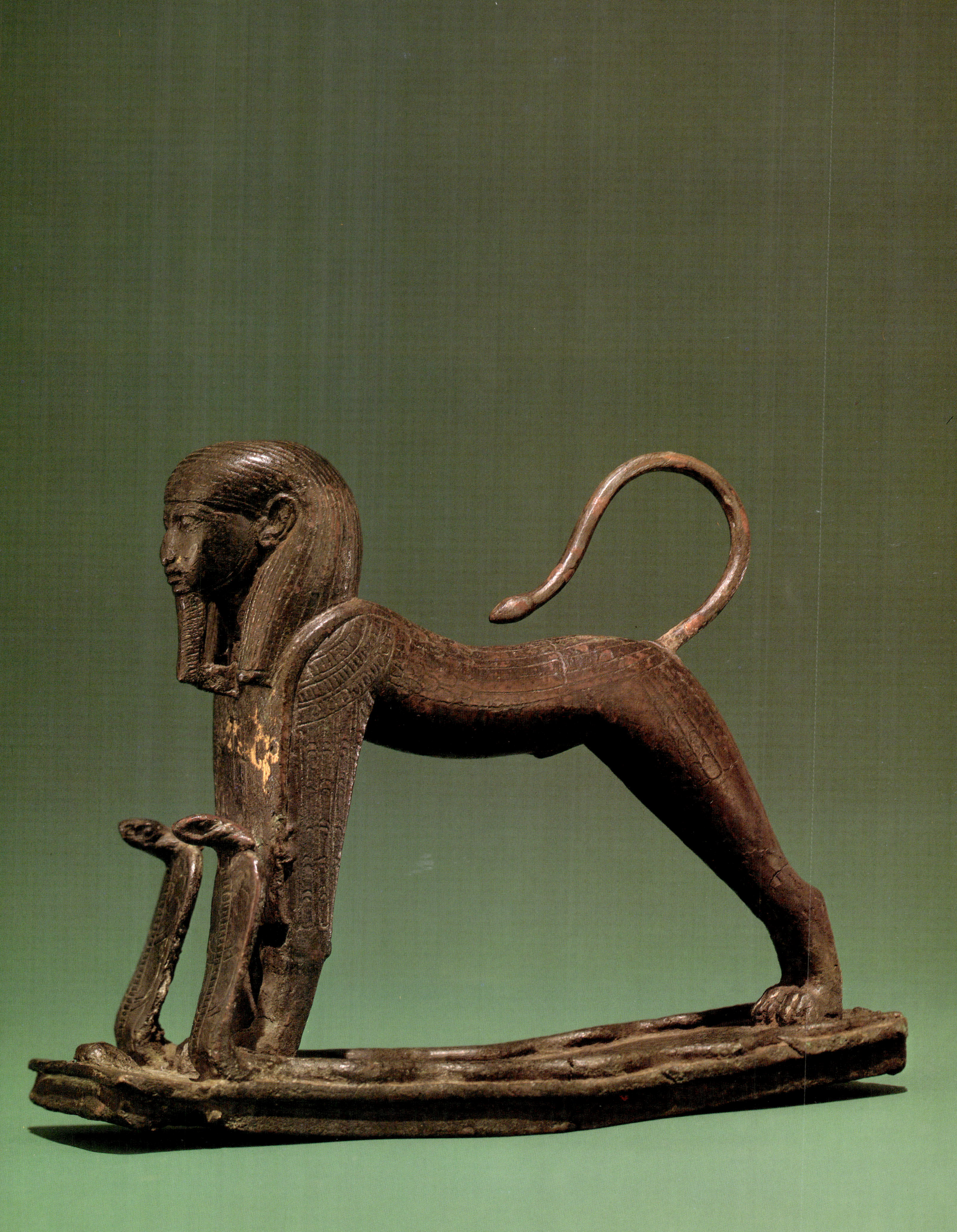

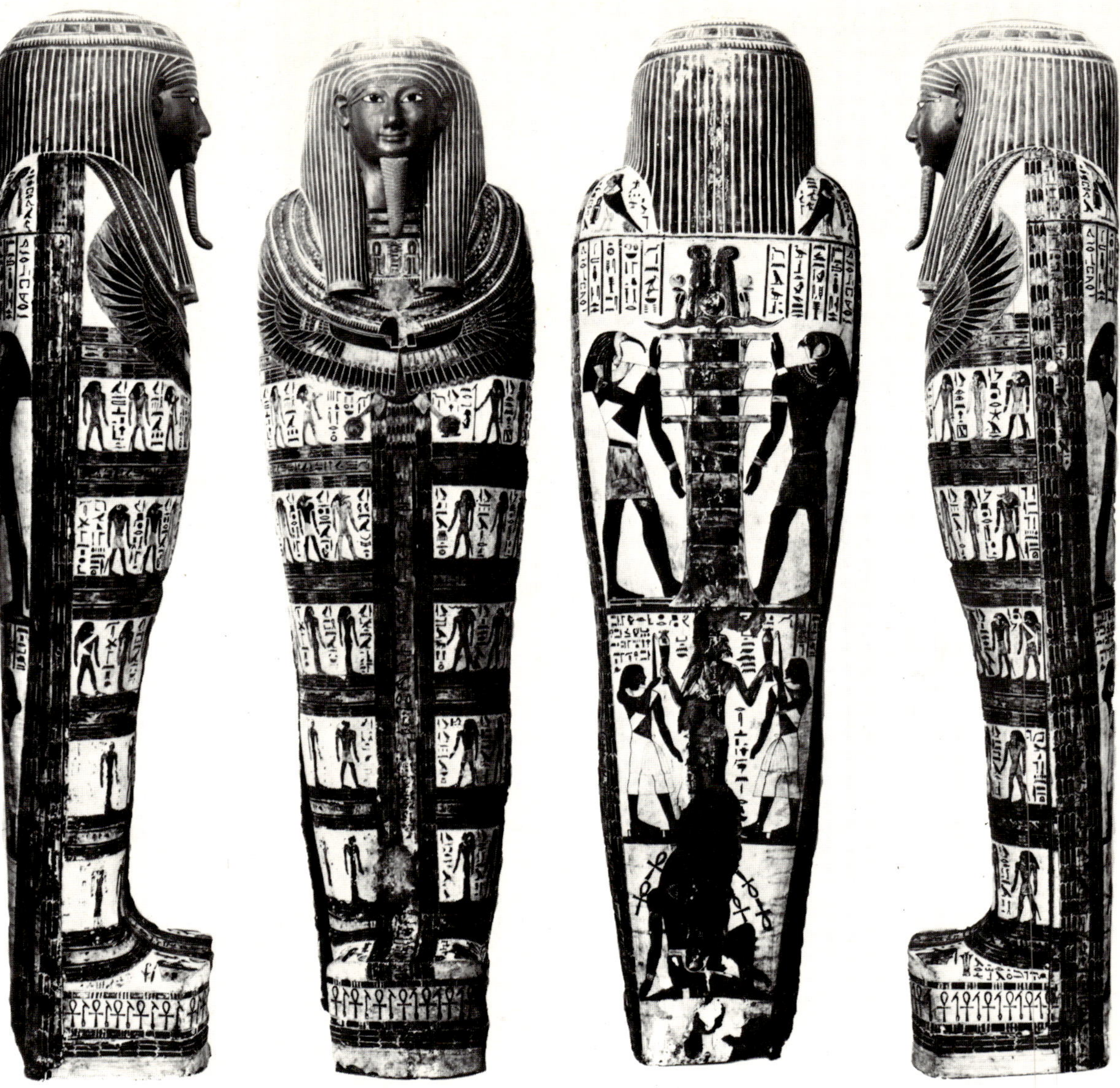

13. Cartonnage of the Priest Nespaneterenpera

Most probably from Thebes
Dynasty XXI, time of the Priest King Pinedjem II, 980–960 B.C.
Cartonnage, lapis lazuli, and glass
Charles Edwin Wilbour Fund, 35.1265
The Brooklyn Museum
1.77 meters (5' 9⅝") in length

Egyptian dead were well prepared for the Afterlife. Embalmed and swathed
in linen wrappings, the mummies were then placed into sarcophagi, which
could be made of stone, wood, or cartonnage. Cartonnage is similar to
papier-mâché and was made by alternating layers of linen or papyrus with
gesso, a kind of plaster. Easily shaped and decorated, cartonnage was often
brilliantly painted and inlaid with glass, faience, and metals.

This handsome cartonnage was one of three which, like Chinese boxes,
contained the mummy of Nespaneterenpera, fourth prophet of Amun and
priest in the city of Hermonthis. The workmanship is of an exceptionally
high quality: the strands of the false beard and hair are executed with great
care; the eyebrows and rims of each eye are inlaid with lapis lazuli; the eyes
themselves are glass.

Tombs for nonroyal, private persons at Thebes during Dynasty XXI were
usually small, simple rooms without decoration on their walls. Therefore,
the prayers and spells necessary to insure the proper completion of the
elaborate funerary rituals were depicted on the cartonnage. Here, the most
remarkable decoration is the broad collar in the shape of a winged ram, a
manifestation of the state god Amun, which spreads across the chest.
Interestingly, this collar has the same shape and function as the priceless
sheet gold collar of the same figure found on the famous mummy of
Tutankhamen.

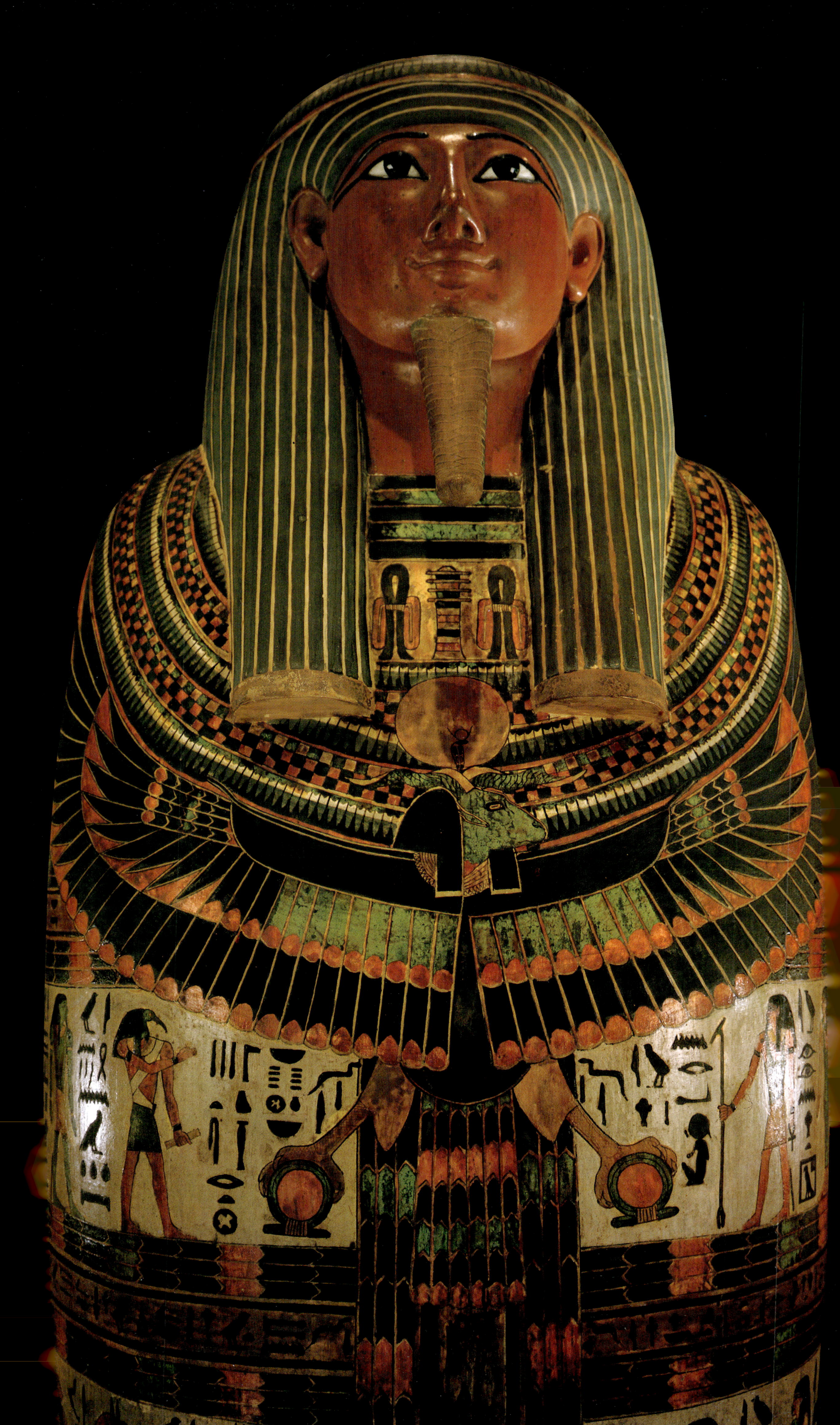

14. Statuette of the God Amun

Reportedly from Minjeh, near Luxor
Dynasty XXV, 745–655 B.C.
Bronze, carnelian, lapis lazuli, and glass paste
Charles Edwin Wilbour Fund, 37.4
The Brooklyn Museum
33.8 cm. (13¹/₄″) in height

The god Amun is here represented in the classical attitude of the striding
male figure with his left foot advanced. He wears a striated kilt, called a
shendyt, and a broad collar over his upper chest. The straps which held
the now missing ceremonial beard in place can still be seen on his cheeks.
His headdress consists of a brimless wicker top hat from which protrude
two feathers and a representation of a sun disk. His right fist originally held
a scepter.

Statuettes such as these were often purchased as votive offerings by
Egyptians before they visited their temples. Once in the sanctuary, the
worshiper would ceremonially present the figure to his deity in hopes
of a wish to be granted or in repayment for a past favor.

The god Amun was particularly popular during Dynasty XXV, when his
sanctuary at Karnak flourished. Many people were named after him, and
many men were called Nespekashuty, which means "The-one-who-belongs-
to-him-who-is-tall-of-feathers," an allusion to the plumes of Amun's
headdress. This statuette of the god is the only bronze representation to
have survived from Ancient Egypt with the name "Amun" in hieroglyphs on
the base.

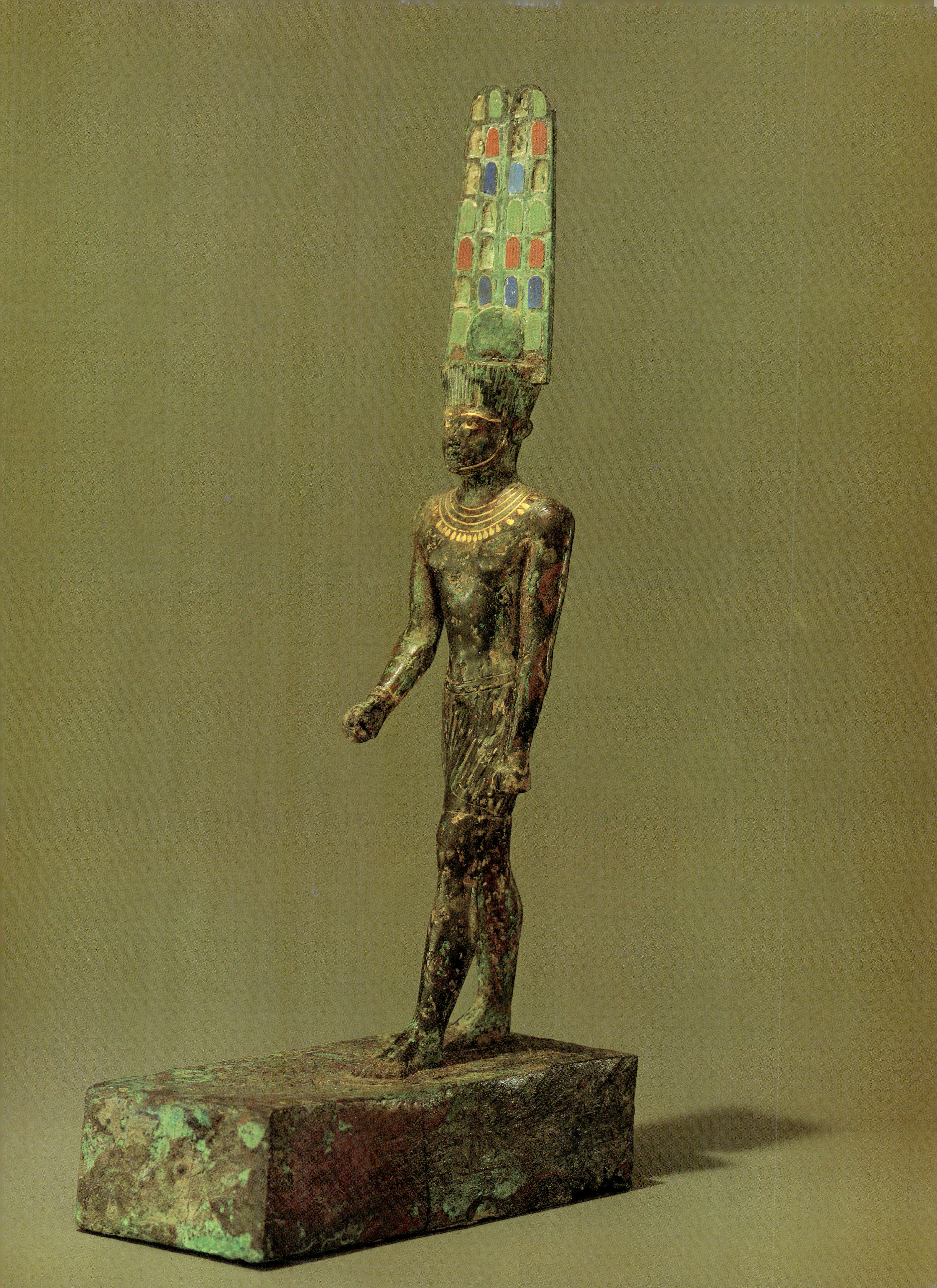

15. Statue of a Cat of the Goddess Bastet

Reportedly from Saqqara
Late Period, 745–342 B.C.
Wood, gilded gesso, bronze, blue glass, and rock crystal
Charles Edwin Wilbour Fund, 37.1945E
The Brooklyn Museum
67.2 cm. (26¹/₂″) in height

Although the ancient Egyptians associated the cat with a number of deities,
by the tenth century B.C. the animal was revered as the incarnation of the
goddess Bastet, patron deity of the city of Bubastis, which means "The
Place of the Ointment." This reference is to the unguents and aromatic
resins used during embalming practices. Another animal god, the
jackal-headed Anubis, when represented as the son of Bastet, is often
called "The Horus of the Sweet Odors."

 This wooden sculpture of a cat of Bastet is extremely naturalistic in its
modeling and is one of the five largest such figures to have survived from
Ancient Egypt. There is a slight depression in its forehead into which a blue
glass scarab, symbol of the sun god as creator of life, has been placed.

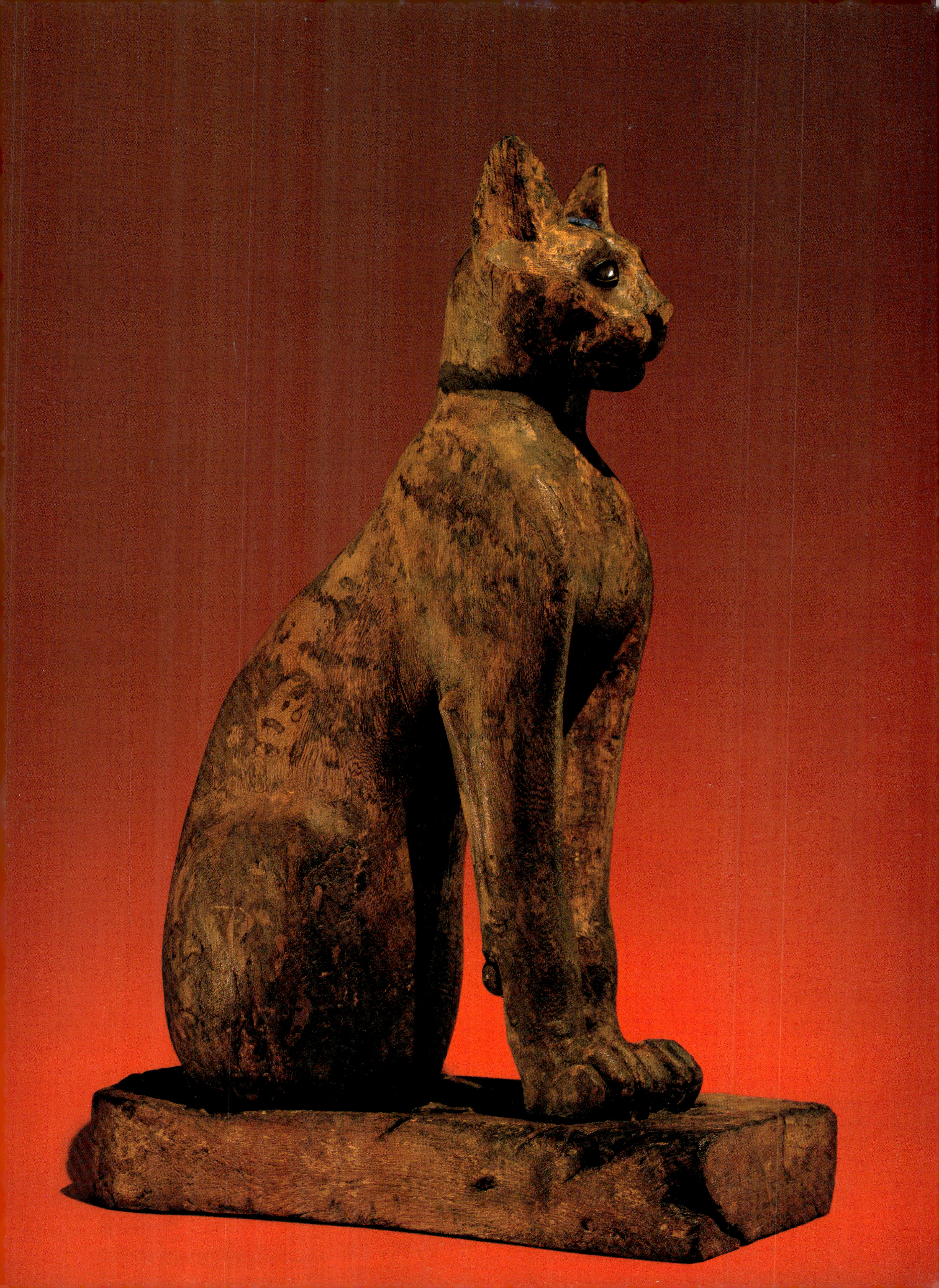

16. Statuette of a Falcon

Provenance not known
Dynasty XXVI, 664–525 B.C.
Bronze and gold
Museum's Collection Fund, 05.394
The Brooklyn Museum
28.8 cm. (11³/₈″) in height

To the ancient Egyptians, the falcon represented Horus, son of Osiris. After Osiris was murdered by his brother Seth, Horus avenged his father and succeeded him on the throne. Subsequently, each pharaoh sought an identification with Horus in an attempt to give his reign legitimacy as the rightful successor of his father. Horus wears the Double Crown consisting of the Red Crown of Lower Egypt, made of wicker, into which is set the cone-shaped White Crown of Upper Egypt, presumably made of leather. A coil protrudes from the base of that crown. On the front of the Red Crown is a uraeus—the royal cobra which protects the king, because, according to legend, its lidless eyes never close.

On this figure the delicate modeling and incised details, particularly the feather pattern on the wings, are consummately crafted. Here, too, is an example of the peculiarly Egyptian technique of inlaying bronze with gold; the eyes are inlaid with gold rims.

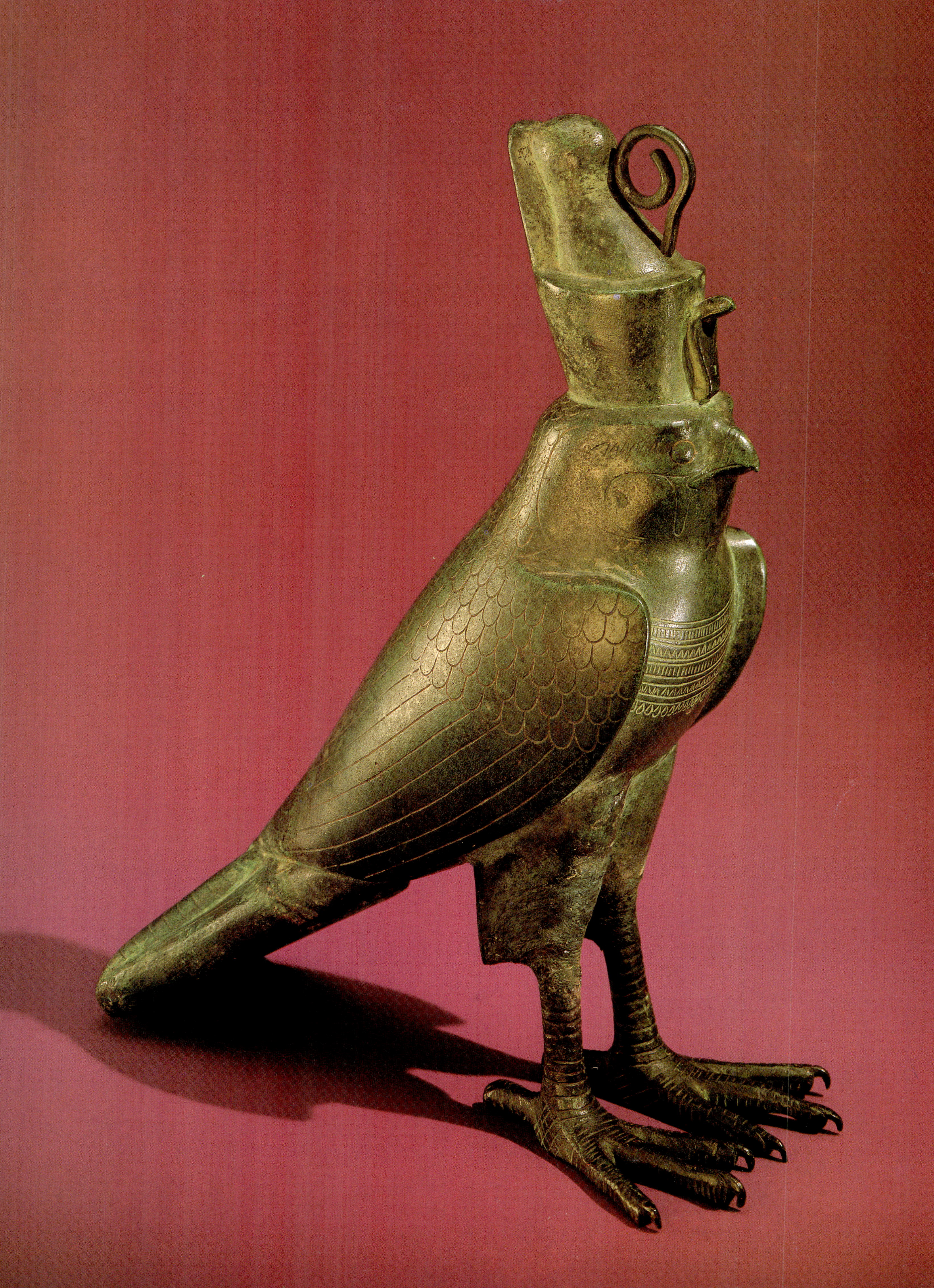

17. Statuette of the *Ba* (Soul) of Pe

From Memphis
Dynasty XXVI, 664–525 B.C.
Bronze
Charles Edwin Wilbour Fund, 37.420E
The Brooklyn Museum
16 cm. (6¹/₄″) in height

During the Predynastic Period (4000–3000 B.C.), Egypt was divided into
two kingdoms. At that time, the city of Buto, in the Delta, was the capital
of Lower Egypt. Within Buto was a district called Pe, which was the center
for the worship of the falcon-headed god Horus. The most distinguishing
features of the cult at Pe were the equation of the falcon-god with the *ba,*
or soul, of the king and its association with the *heb-sed,* or jubilee festival.
At regular intervals (in principle every thirty years but actually more
frequently than that), the king performed the *heb-sed* to insure his
rejuvenation.

   This particular bronze is associated with that festival and is actually
a three-dimensional representation of the hieroglyph *henu,* meaning
"jubilation." In the Egyptian tradition the emotion was expressed by
shouting accompanied by striking the chest with alternating fists—a
gesture best known to a modern audience as appropriate to Tarzan.

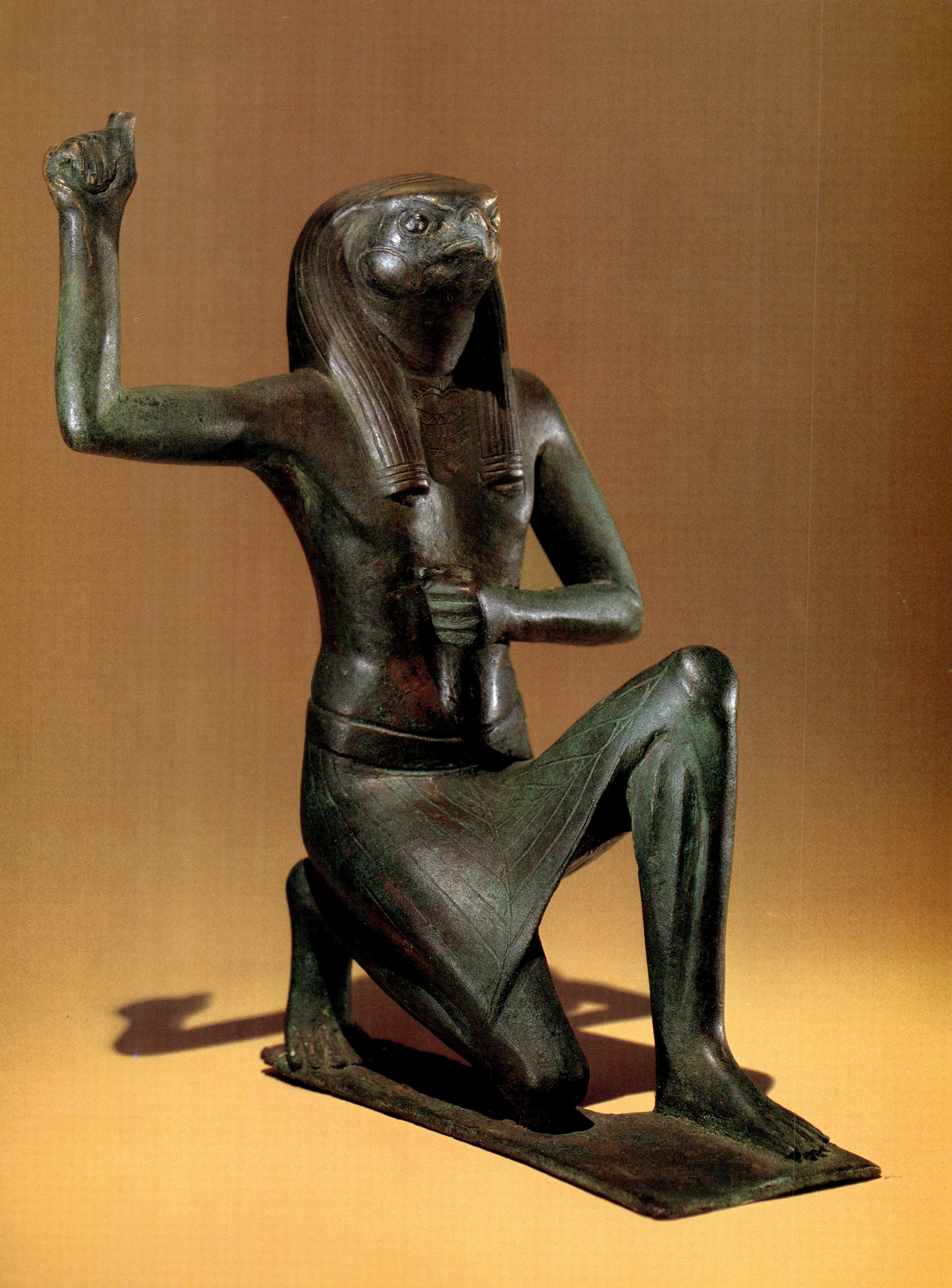

18. Seated Lion with an Alabastron

Probably from Leontopolis
Dynasty XXVII [The First Persian Period], 525–404 B.C.
Calcite or Egyptian alabaster
Charles Edwin Wilbour Fund, 53.223
The Brooklyn Museum
10.6 cm. (4¹/₈″) in height

After the Persian king Cambyses conquered Egypt in 525 B.C., many
Egyptian craftsmen created novel forms to attract the patronage of their
new masters. One such creation was a luxurious vessel of the kind pictured
here, a cosmetic jar which is a masked allusion to the principal deities of
the Greek-named Egyptian city of Leontopolis. The place, whose name
literally means "City of the Lion," was sacred to Maahes, the Lion God.
Here, the figure of the lion holds an alabastron, or ointment jar, which
originally contained an expensive aromatic unguent manufactured at
Leontopolis. The perfume itself was sacred to Nefertum, the other popular
deity of that city.

Such vessels were probably manufactured as souvenirs for wealthy
Persian tourists who visited Leontopolis. The inlays of this piece are now
missing, but are a characteristic of Persian art which the Egyptian
craftsmen adapted to appeal to Persian tastes.

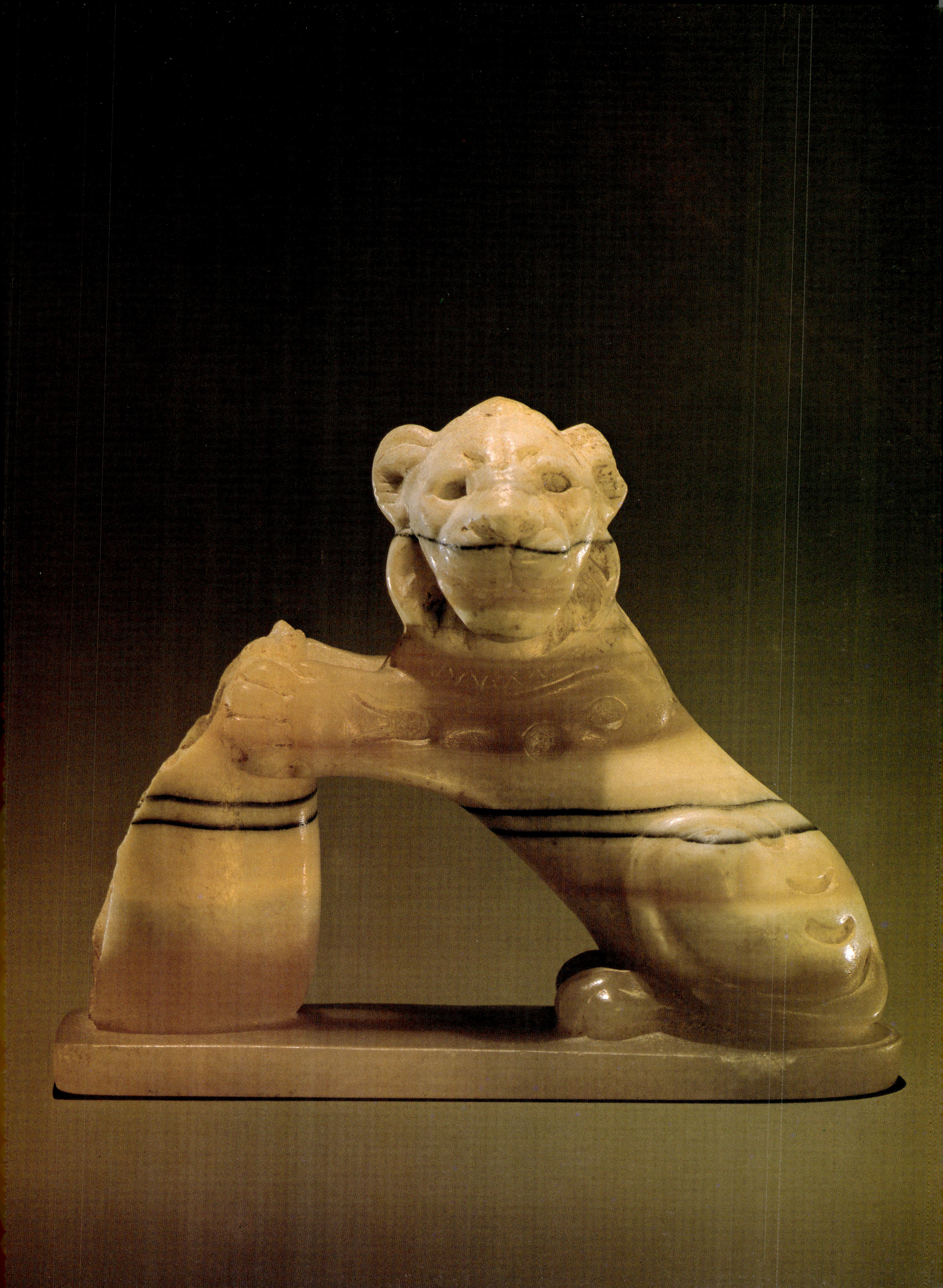

19. Spacer

From Meroë
Napatan Period, reign of King Amtalqa, 568–555 B.C.
Sheet gold
Charles Edwin Wilbour Fund, 49.29
The Brooklyn Museum
4.55 cm. (1³/₄") in height

Combining beauty of form with practical function, this elegant small object was strung on a necklace in order to keep its seven individual strands from becoming entangled with one another. It is inscribed for King Amtalqa, who ruled an independent kingdom south of Aswan. The carefully cut hieroglyphs translate, "The Son of Ra, the Lord of Diadems, Amtalqa, may he live forever! The one who is beloved of the goddess Hathor, the Mistress of Heliopolis, the Mistress of the Gods, who gives life." This inscription indicates that the necklace to which this spacer belonged was actually worn by King Amtalqa.

It is interesting to note that Amtalqa's kingdom is presently referred to as Nubia, a word which derives from the Egyptian hieroglyph for "gold," since most of the ore was imported from that region by the ancient Egyptians.

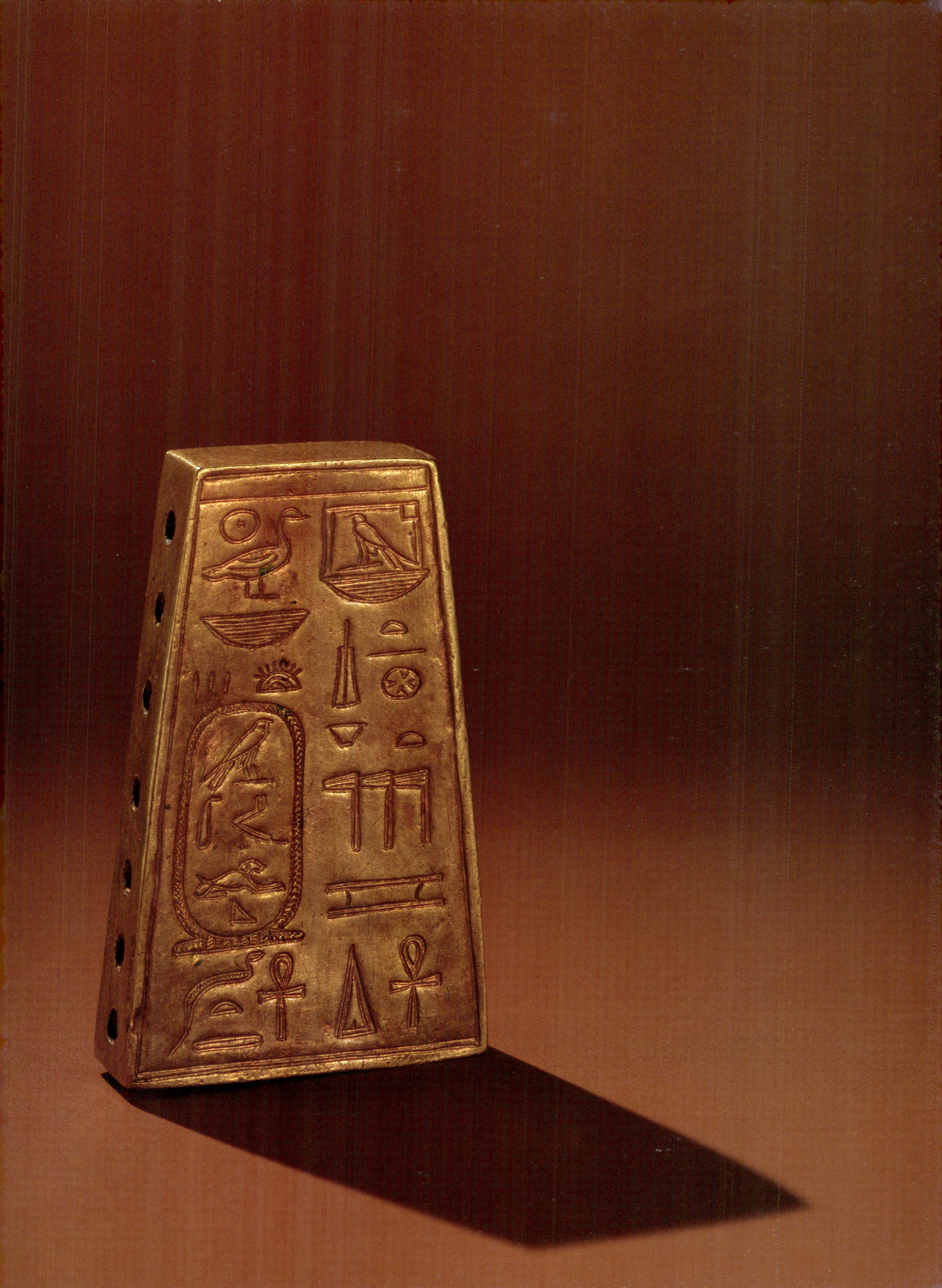

20. Head from a Statue of Wesir-wer

From the Cachette at Karnak
Dynasty XXX, 380–342 B.C.
Metamorphic schist
Charles Edwin Wilbour Fund, 55.175
The Brooklyn Museum
15 cm. (5⁷/₈″) in height

The recent history of this fine portrait is a fascinating example of art historical scholarship—a kind of detective story that illustrates what curators and scholars can do with time, the generous exchange of information, and freedom from the demands of administrative red tape.

This head has been known to Egyptologists since the early part of the century. On a flat pillar at its back are traces of an inscription which scholars meticulously recorded. But little else was known, and there was no sign at all of the body from which the head had come.

Meanwhile, in the Cairo Museum stood a headless statue, which had been among more than two thousand sculptures discovered in an excavation in 1903 at the site of the Temple of Karnak by the French Egyptologist Georges Legrain. The pieces had evidently been buried by priests of the Temple of Amun in one of their periodic house cleanings in which they disposed of older sculptures to make way for new.

During the course of a continuing study of Late Egyptian sculpture, an Italian scholar compared the recorded inscriptions on both the head and the torso. And she concluded that they belonged together, an opinion that has since been confirmed by a series of measurements and precise analysis of the materials of both parts. Only a hypothetical reconstruction is now possible since the Cairo Museum owns the lower part.

As a result of this international scholarly collaboration, we know that Wesir-wer was a prophet of the gods Amun and Montu at Thebes, where he served as governor and as a treasury official. The individualistic features of his face convey a sense of duty and responsibility and demonstrate the ability of Egyptian artists to capture precise likenesses in stone.

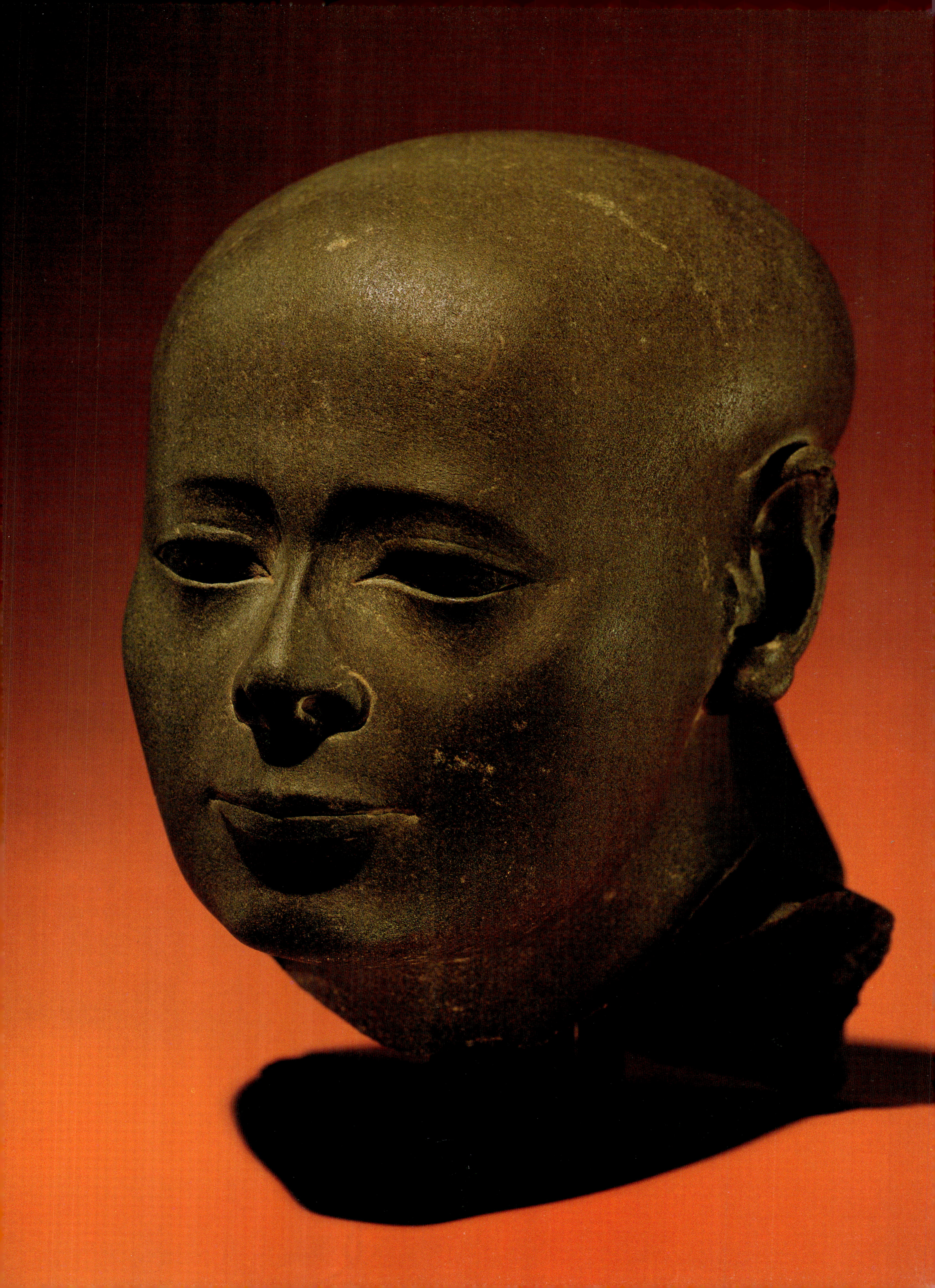

21. Head of the God Osiris

Provenance not known
Ptolemaic Period, 305–30 B.C.
Wood, gilded gesso, bronze, and glass
Charles Edwin Wilbour Fund, 58.94
The Brooklyn Museum
36.2 cm. (14¹/₄″) in height

This dramatic head of the major god of the Afterlife, Osiris, demonstrates
how Egyptian craftsmen incorporated various materials into one object.
The surfaces of the carefully carved wood were covered with gesso, a finely
textured plaster. This coating was then gilded. The body of the royal uraeus
(the serpent over the brow), the beard, and the rims of the eyes were then
added in bronze. Details in the body of the uraeus and the eyes of Osiris
were completed in glass. The result is a very colorful, "mixed media"
sculpture.

   Osiris was traditionally represented as a mummified human. Legend
recalls how Osiris was dismembered by his brother and arch-rival Seth, the
god of natural disasters, and how he was put back together again, like
Humpty Dumpty, by his faithful consort Isis. Osiris's death and subsequent
rebirth held out the hope of salvation to all Egyptians, regardless of their
status in life. Consequently, the cult of Osiris became extremely popular
among the lower classes of the Egyptian population. The site of Abydos, the
center of Osiris worship, can be compared to the great religious centers of
the Middle Ages and, like them, attracted tens of thousands of zealous
pilgrims annually.

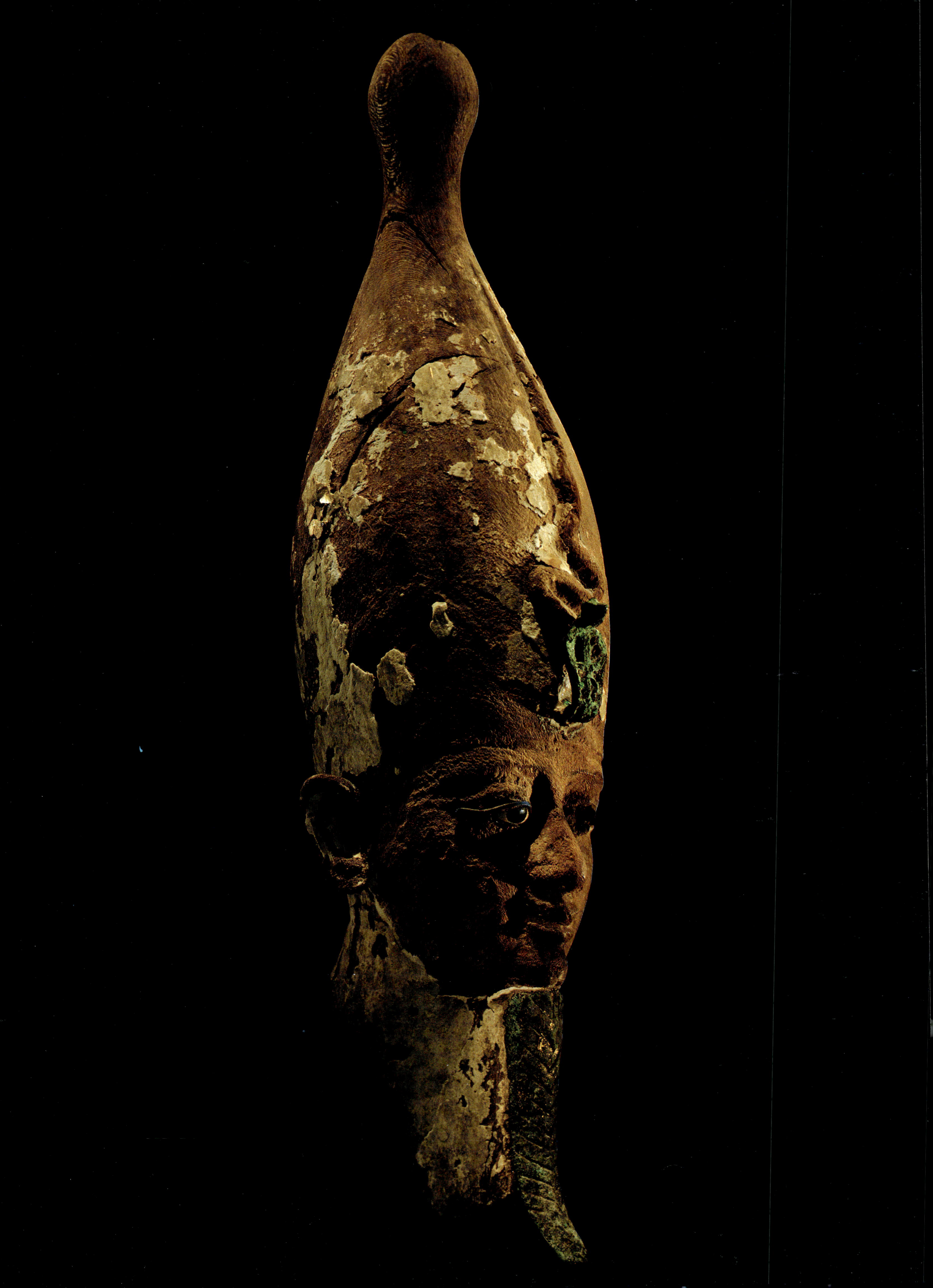

22. Figure of an Ibis

From the Ibis Cemetery at Tuna el Gebel, near Tell el Amarna
Ptolemaic Period, 305–30 B.C.
Gilded wood, gold, silver, and natural crystal
Charles Edwin Wilbour Fund, 49.48
The Brooklyn Museum
41.8 cm. (16^1/$_2$") in length

During the Ptolemaic Period, native Egyptians, confronted by the customs of their Greek rulers, reverted to worshiping their deities in primeval, animal forms. As an expression of this aspect of their piety, the Egyptians established numerous animal cemeteries near important cult centers throughout Egypt. At Tuna el Gebel, the cult site of Thoth—who was represented here as an ibis—lies a vast subterranean network of catacombs into whose walls literally thousands of mummified ibises were interred. Many of these mummies were placed in ibis-shaped coffins.

This exquisitely realistic statuette of an ibis is actually one of those coffins. Its body is hollow; a lid on its back could be removed and the mummy placed inside. Such objects were left as offerings to Thoth by pious pilgrims.

This example is of extraordinary workmanship and is perhaps the only complete figure of this type whose legs, neck, head, and bill are crafted from solid silver: the glass eyes have rims of solid gold. Such a splendid object could only have been made for one of the wealthiest Egyptians of the time.

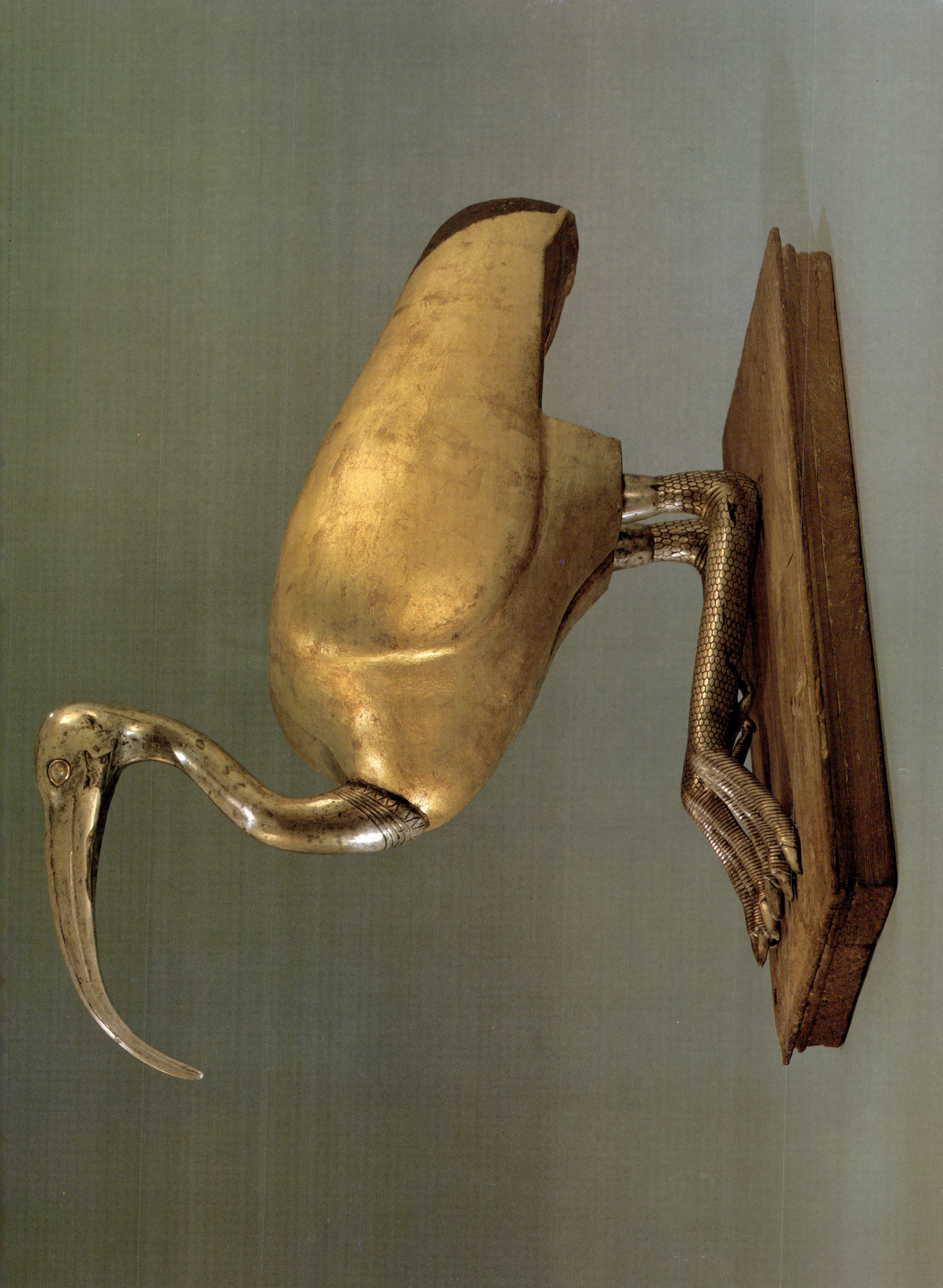

23. Figure of a Cynocephalous Ape

Provenance not known
Ptolemaic Period, 305–30 B.C.
Pale green faience
Charles Edwin Wilbour Fund, 36.838
The Brooklyn Museum
10.3 cm. (4") in height

Many of the objects that have come down to us from Ancient Egypt seem to be perfectly straightforward representations of natural beings or to have a simple decorative function. But often they conceal a cryptographic message. Such is the case with this faience figure of a baboon. The animal represents the Egyptian word for "writing." Here, it is depicted crouching on a *heb*-sign, which stands for the word "Lord." By means of a complex and sophisticated system of puns, evolved during the Ptolemaic Period, the form and content of the work evoke a hieroglyphic phrase which translates as "The Lord of Writing." This allusion is, of course, to the god Thoth, to whom the baboon was sacred.

Faience, the material of this elegant piece, is a term loosely applied to a quartz paste that was cast in molds and fired in kilns to produce a highly glazed surface. Although objects of Egyptian faience are customarily blue, examples in yellow and green, like this figure, are well known. The sculptured molds for the figures were used over and over, but with each use the details of each casting would become blurred through wear. The exceptionally crisp details on this example, particularly evident in the mane and muzzle, indicate that the piece was among the first ones cast from its mold. It is reasonable to assume that this handsome small figurine was appropriately dedicated to Thoth, his personal deity, by an Egyptian scribe.

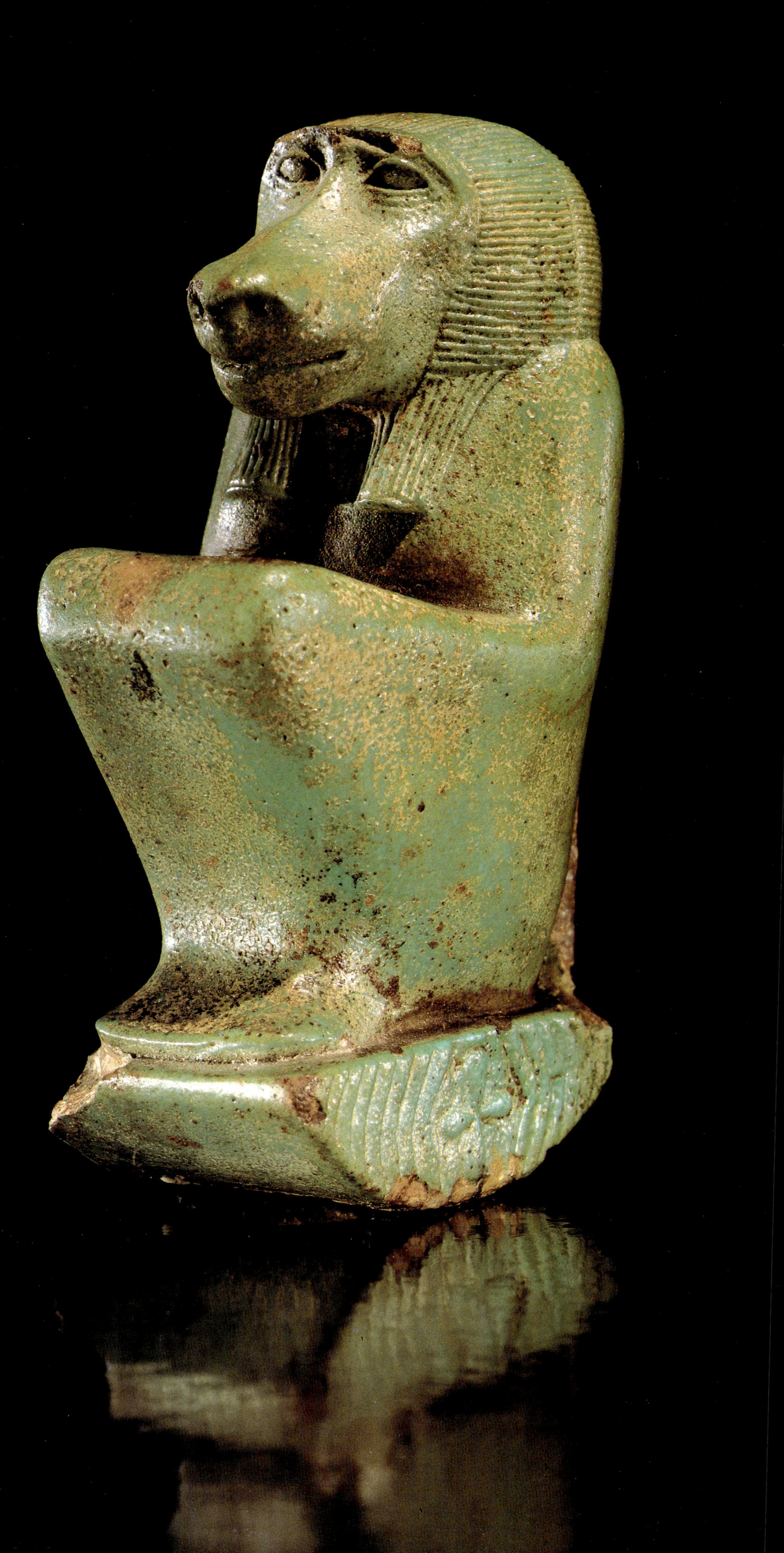

24. Amulet of a *Ba*-Bird

From Saqqara
Ptolemaic Period, 305–30 B.C.
Gold with inlays of lapis lazuli, turquoise, and steatite
Charles Edwin Wilbour Fund, 37.804E
The Brooklyn Museum
6 cm. (2⅝″) in width

It is difficult to find contemporary terms which are exact equivalents of
ancient Egyptian concepts. Nowhere is this difficulty more evident than
in attempting a definition of the Egyptian concept of the *ba,* which is
conveniently translated "soul," but must be understood without the
Christian overtones of that word. To the ancient Egyptians, *ba* was a
manifestation of the deceased which appeared as a human-headed bird.
Buried with its human host, the *ba* could escape from the body, leave the
tomb, and flutter about the earth beneath the rays of the sun. This freedom
was, however, short-lived since the *ba* was forced to return to be reunited
with the mummified corpse of the deceased. The survival of the *ba* and its
corpse was essential for the survival of the deceased in the Hereafter.

Amulets depicting the *ba* came into vogue during Dynasty XXVI
(664–525 B.C.) when they were made of simple pieces of sheet gold. By the
time of the Ptolemaic Period, the *ba*-bird amulet had evolved into a jewel.
During embalming, a series of such amulets might be strung together on
one strand of a broad collar which was then placed around the upper chest
of the deceased.

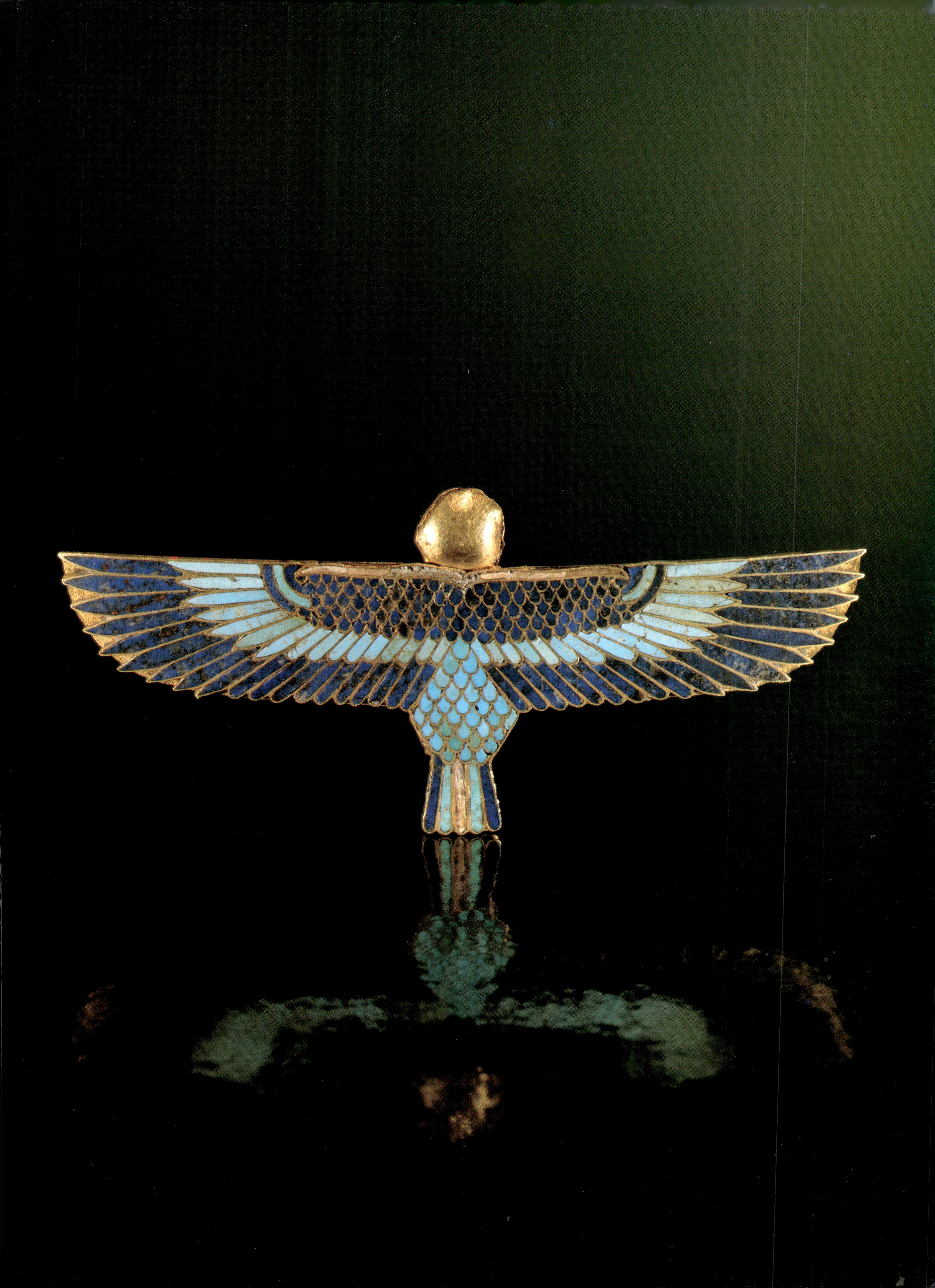

25. Figure of the Goddess Isis

Provenance not known
Early Ptolemaic Period, 305–221 B.C.
Blue, glassy faience
Charles Edwin Wilbour Fund, 37.332E
The Brooklyn Museum
7 cm. (2³/₄″) in height

By the time of the Ptolemaic Period, the goddess Isis had eclipsed all other
Egyptian goddesses in importance. Her cult was even exported beyond
Egypt, and sanctuaries to her were dedicated throughout Greece and Italy.
The appeal of Isis rested primarily on her familial characteristics, as the
faithful consort of Osiris and loving mother of their offspring Horus.
Originally, this faience figure of Isis was part of a group which represented
her seated on a throne, holding the child Horus, whom she was nursing,
on her lap. The fecundity expressed by this act of a mother goddess is
emphasized in the exuberance of her anatomy and heightened by the tightly
fitting sheath she wears, which also conveys a sense of nudity. This interest
in the female figure is a typically Egyptian characteristic, as comparison
with representations of women from the earlier Dynasty XVIII (1554-
1305 B.C.) reveals. The presence of Greeks in Egypt during the Ptolemaic
Period had little effect on native craftsmen, who remained true to their
millennia-old artistic conventions.

   The particularly realistic details of this sculpture have also aided in
dating it. Here, the delicately modeled face with straight, natural brows, the
thin nose, and the gently smiling lips with their drilled corners imbue the
figure with the traits of Queen Arsinoe II, who ruled from 275 to 270 B.C.
On the basis of these similarities, this figure of Isis seems reliably
attributable to the first half of the Ptolemaic Period.

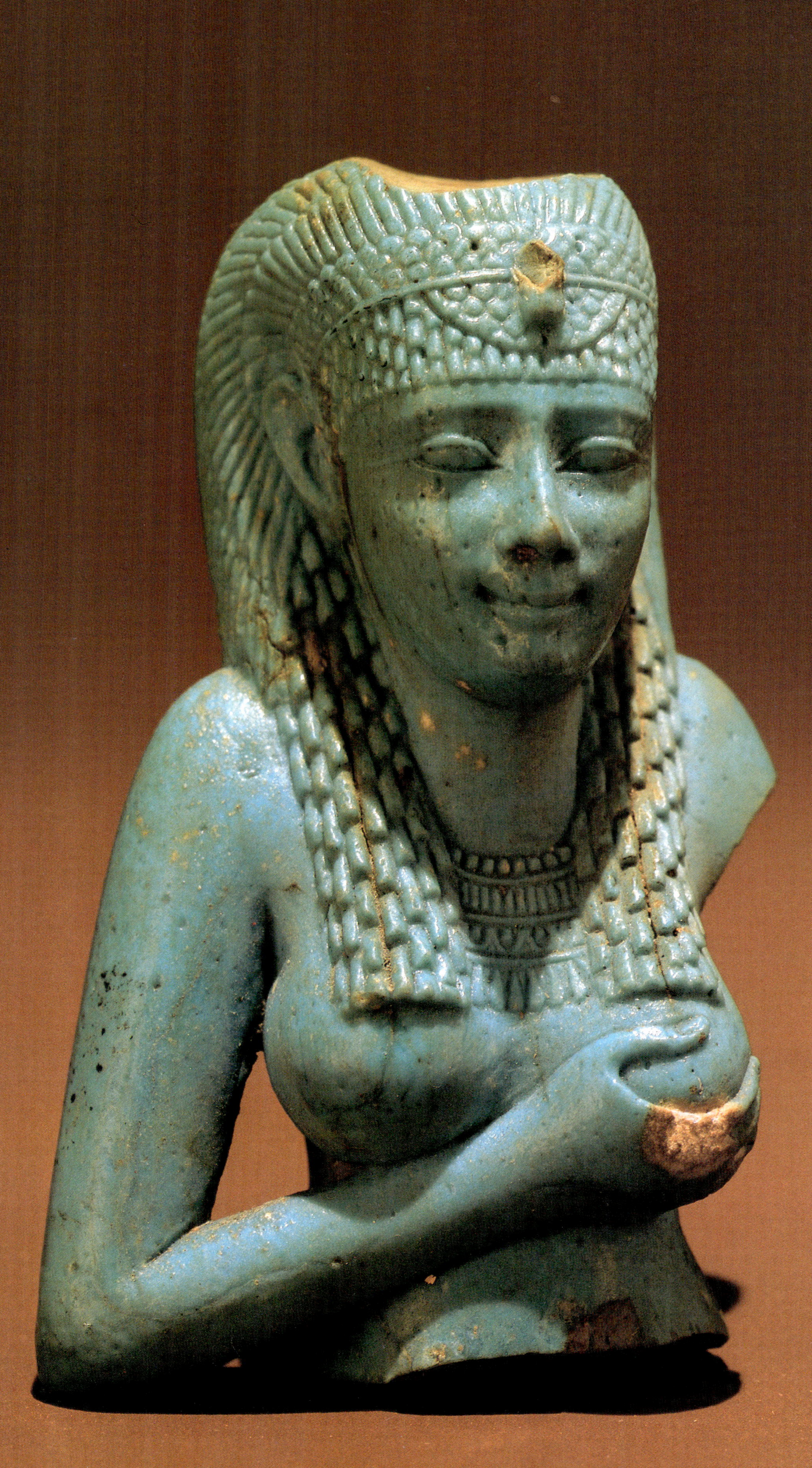

26. Statuette of the God Thoth

Tuna el Gebel, near Tell el Amarna
Ptolemaic Period, 305–30 B.C.
Green faience
Charles Edwin Wilbour Fund, 51.229
The Brooklyn Museum
16.8 cm. (6⅝") in height

This delicately detailed statuette represents the god Thoth, Lord of Writing
and Patron of Scribes, who, as other examples have shown, were fond of puns
in the Ptolemaic Period. One of these puns is visually represented here.
Egyptian legend regarded the moon as the eye of the god Horus. When the
moon waned each month, the eye of Horus was thought to have become ill.
The god Thoth healed the eye, and thereby brought about the occurrence
of the full or new moon. To indicate Thoth's role in this process, he is here
shown holding the hieroglyph for "to be hale/uninjured." This is also the
same sign for the eye of Horus. Consequently, Thoth is shown with the
uninjured eye of Horus, which he is bringing back to the heavens. Two
protective spirits, whose heads appear at Thoth's feet, escort and protect
him from evil.

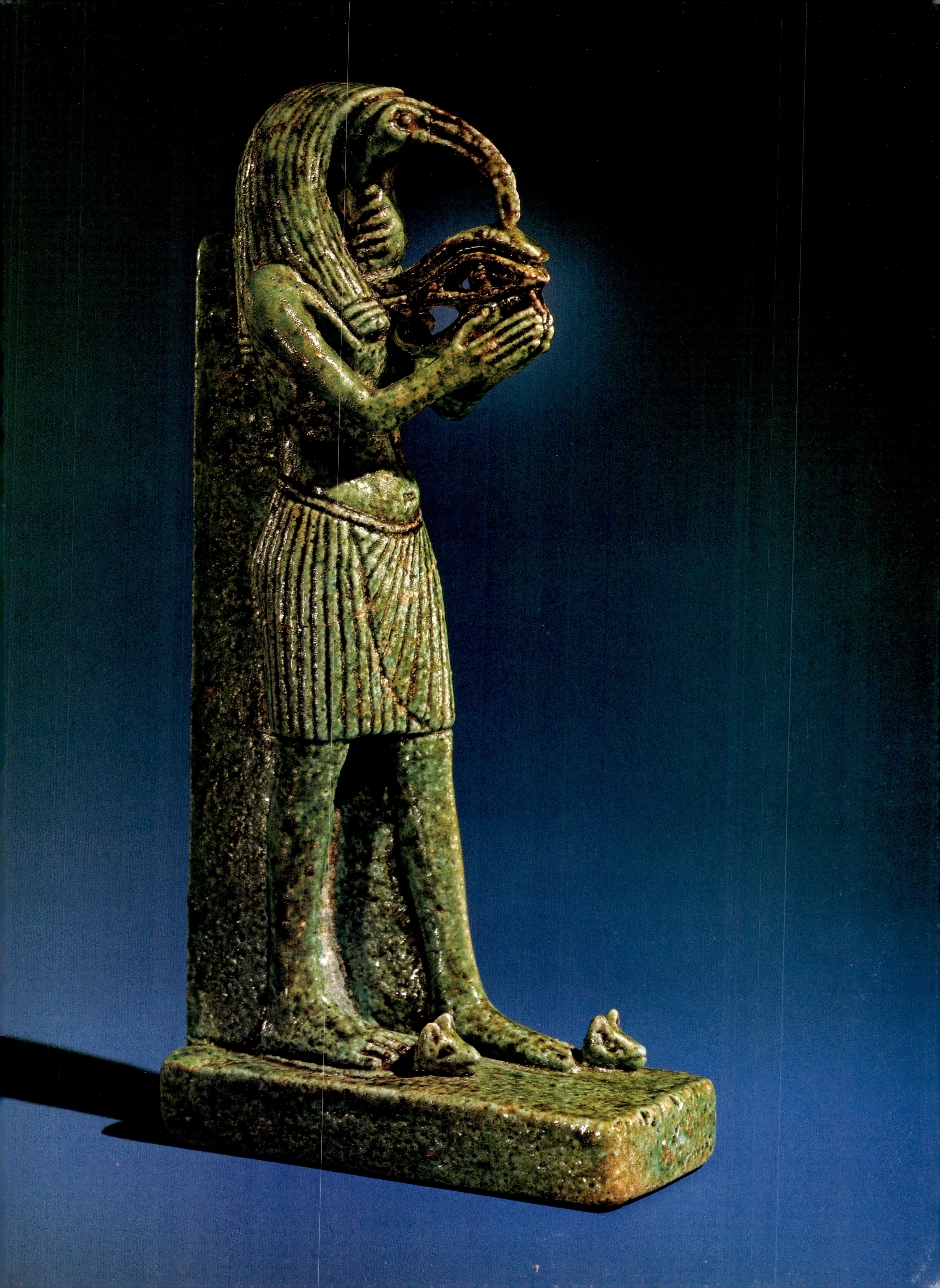

27. Figure of the Deity Nemesis

Reportedly from Akhmim
Roman Period, Second Century A.D.
Blue faience
Charles Edwin Wilbour Fund, 53.173
The Brooklyn Museum
23.4 cm. (9¹/₄″) in height

This composite beast, with the beak of a falcon, long, pointed ears of a
feline, body of a lion, breasts of a woman, and recurved wings is a griffin.
Known from very early Egyptian representations, the griffin was associated
with the deity Nemesis by the Greeks who settled in Egypt in large numbers
after Alexander the Great conquered Egypt in 332 B.C. Nemesis was a
peculiar deity who personified the disapproval of the gods for human
presumption. The Greeks thought that prosperity accompanied by
unbridled pride would often be followed by reverses of the worst sort. If
one was suddenly fortunate, therefore, it was sensible to try to forestall the
wrath of Nemesis by propitiating her. Here, Nemesis's right paw rests on the
Wheel of Fortune—a reminder of the fickle whims of Fate.

   In this statuette, the blue faience is highlighted by black in the pupil of
the eye and yellow in the necklace and nipples. This combination of colors
in faience is typical for works created at various sites throughout Egypt in
the second century A.D.

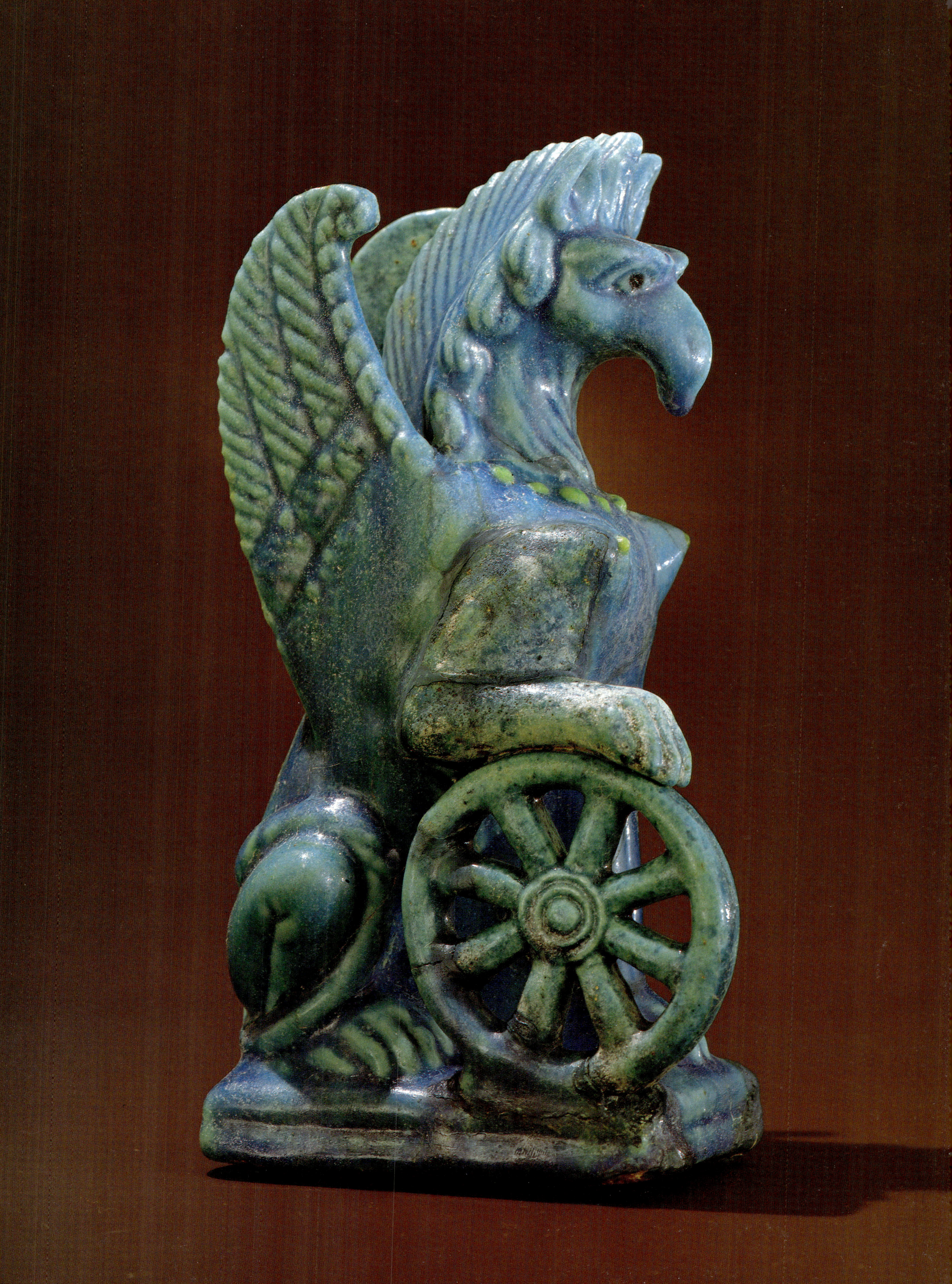

28. Mummy Cartonnage of a Woman

From Hawara, in the Fayum
First Century A.D.
Gilded cartonnage and glass
Charles Edwin Wilbour Fund, 69.35
The Brooklyn Museum
57.6 cm. (22⅝″) in height

This elegant cartonnage contained the mummy of an unidentified, but
obviously wealthy, woman. The elaborate ensemble of jewelry is known
from actual examples excavated in Egypt. She wears a fringed shawl
knotted over the right breast—the traditional costume of Isis, consort of
Osiris, one of the most popular of Egyptian goddesses. This dress equates
the woman with Isis and guarantees her eternal life, as does the hand-held
corsage made of rose petals. Since gold does not tarnish, its color soon
became equated with incorruptibility and permanence. The gilding,
therefore, reinforced the idea of the eternal preservation of the mummy
which was encased by the cartonnage.

An interesting sidelight in the use of cartonnage is that during the
Roman Period, from which this handsome object comes, it was common to
substitute old papyrus documents for linen in making cartonnage. As a
consequence, specialists have often meticulously disassembled these works
of art in order to recover the papyri, some of which have been discovered
to contain lost literary works.

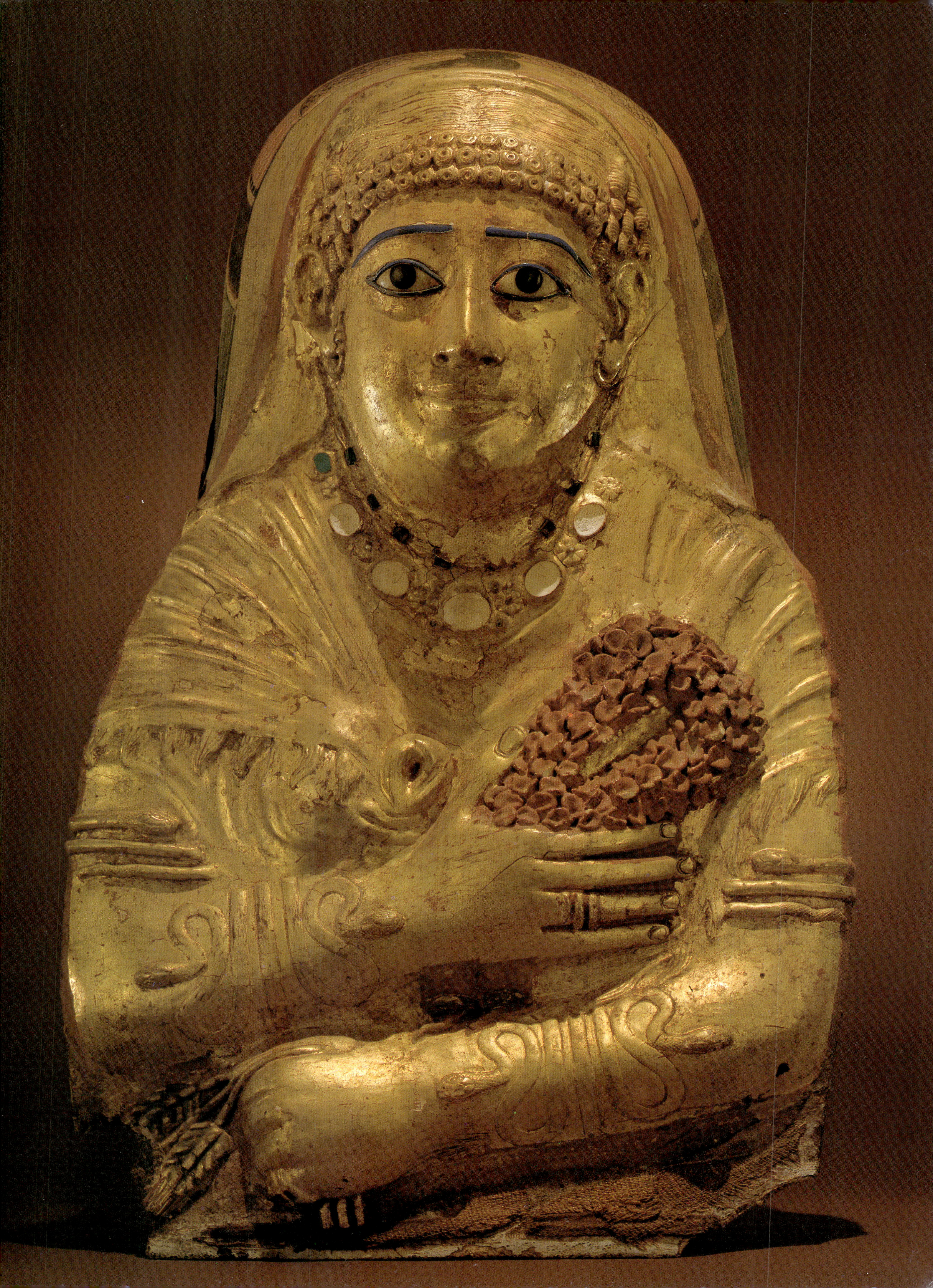